Me Jewel and Darlin' Dublin

50ᵀᴴ ANNIVERSARY EDITION

Éamonn MacThomáis (13 January 1927–16 August 2002) was an author, broadcaster, historian, Irish Republican, advocate of the Irish language and lecturer. He presented his own series on Dublin on RTÉ during the 1970s and was well known for guided tours of and lectures on his beloved Dublin. Éamonn died in 2002 and is buried in Dublin's Glasnevin Cemetery.

ME JEWEL AND DARLIN' DUBLIN

50TH ANNIVERSARY EDITION

ÉAMONN MACTHOMÁIS

ILLUSTRATED BY MICHAEL O'BRIEN

THE O'BRIEN PRESS
DUBLIN

This 50th anniversary edition first published 2024
Originally published 1974 by The O'Brien Press Ltd.,
12 Terenure Road East, Rathgar,
Dublin 6, D06 HD27, Ireland.
Tel: +353 1 4923333; Fax: +353 1 4922777
E-mail: books@obrien.ie
Website: obrien.ie

Second edition (revised) 1975, third edition 1977
Reprinted 1980, first paperback edition 1980
Second paperback edition 1983, reprinted 1985, 1988
First revised anniversary edition published 1994.
This edition first published 2024.

The O'Brien Press is a member of Publishing Ireland

ISBN: 978-1-78849-532-5

Text copyright © Éamonn MacThomáis.
Drawings copyright © Michael O'Brien.

The moral rights of the author and illustrator have been asserted.
Copyright for typesetting, layout, editing, design
© The O'Brien Press Ltd
Layout and design by Emma Byrne
Cover illustration by Michael O'Brien

All rights reserved. No part of this publication may be
reproduced or utilised in any form or by any means,
electronic or mechanical, including for text and
data mining, training artificial intelligence systems,
photocopying, recording or in any information storage
and retrieval system, without permission in writing
from the publisher.

8 7 6 5 4 3 2 1
28 27 26 25 24

Printed and bound by Nørhaven Paperback A/S, Denmark.
The paper in this book is produced using pulp from managed forests

Published in
DUBLIN
UNESCO
City of Literature

Great Irish books
O'BRIEN
obrien.ie

FSC
MIX
Paper | Supporting responsible forestry
FSC® C104608

CONTENTS

PUBLISHER'S FOREWORD – IVAN O'BRIEN 7
FOREWORD – DONAL FALLON 11

1 A Child's World
THE FOURPENNY RUSH 15
A DUBLIN PENNY 19
STREET GAMES 21

2 The Old Ways
THE PAWNSHOPS OF DUBLIN 27
THE COMEDY KING 34
STREET CHARACTERS 40
SOME DUBLIN SLANG 51
SOUNDS, SMELLS AND COLOURS 55
DUBLIN'S OLD NEWSPAPERS 60

3 Old Dublin Town
DUBLIN'S MANY LIBERTIES 69
AROUND ST WERBURGH'S 85
FORD OF HURDLES 89

4 Commercial Life
BACK OF THE PIPES 109
MERCHANTS AND MARKETS 112
A TRIP DOWN THE PORT 121

5 Hidden Places
AROUND ST MARY'S ABBEY 127
THE FIVE LAMPS 134
THE ROYAL CIRCUS 140
PHOENIX PARK 144
THE KING'S COWBOY 147
OLD KILMAINHAM 148

6 The City Centre
ST STEPHEN'S GREEN 155
TRINITY COLLEGE 170
AROUND COLLEGE GREEN 176
DUBLIN'S REVOLUTIONARY SQUARE 181

A NOTE ON PUBLICATION 188
INDEX 191

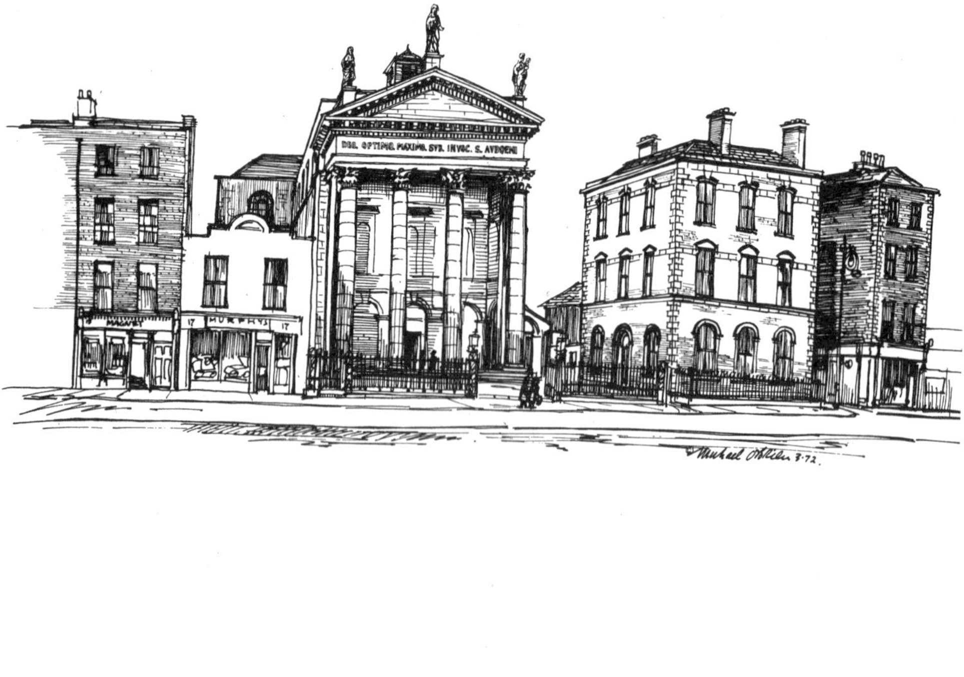
DEO. OPTIMO. MAXIMO. SVB. INVOC. S. AVDOENI
17 MURPHYS 17

Publisher's Foreword by Ivan O'Brien

Dublin was a very different place when *Me Jewel and Darlin' Dublin* was written, back in 1974. The attitude of those in power was dour and unimaginative; they seemed intent on knocking down old buildings, rather than seeing beyond the decay to what lay beneath.

Éamonn MacThomáis saw things differently: having grown up in the south inner city he had a deep affection for the city of his birth. His Republicanism also gave him a different perspective: he wasn't afraid to express pride in the good things his country had. About St George's Church on Hardwicke Street, he writes: 'The spire is a comforting sight, a beautiful sight, from the barred windows of Mountjoy Jail.' As editor of *An Phoblacht*, the Republican newspaper, Éamonn was considered a threat to the state and held for a period without trial. With time to fill he got to 'thinking about my childhood, the people I had met, the places I had seen, about Dublin and its people.'

Tom O'Brien, my grandfather, ran a printing company on Parliament Street. This company was moving towards being a publisher, and Éamonn wrote to Tom (or Tommy, as Éamonn knew him) with an outline of a book that would look back at the Dublin of his youth with affection and humour.

ME JEWEL AND DARLIN' DUBLIN

This was a pretty revolutionary idea in a country in the grip of a seemingly never-ending recession and with the Northern Ireland conflict taking place.

Éamonn picks up the story:

Within a day or two, a young man with a very black beard called to see me. He was, of course, the one and only Michael O'Brien, artist, and son of Tommy. Well, without Tommy the book would never have been written, and without Michael the book would never have been printed and published. Oh, how he fought for my manuscripts at the jail gates. The courage of the father Tommy was well matched by the courage of the son Michael.

And so, with the encouragement and help of his wife Rosaleen, Éamonn allowed his memories to flow and the spirit of the city he loved to make its way onto the page.

Me Jewel and Darlin' Dublin was the first book that The O'Brien Press published. With many illustrations by Michael O'Brien, an activist for the preservation of Dublin's architecture, as well as photographs and other illustration, the production standards were lavish for the time: it was a substantial risk, but one worth taking.

The importance of a native publishing industry to an independent country might seem obvious now, but at the time almost no one was producing books, other than school books, in Ireland. Michael, along with other young turks like Steve McDonagh (Brandon) and Seamus Cashman (Wolfhound) set out to change that, but it wasn't easy. Long used to getting their books from London publishers, some of Dublin's booksellers suggested that there was no need for books to be created here. However, the sales figures (and some of their braver female employees, like Maura Hastings in Eason) soon proved them wrong, and showed that there was a real audience for what Éamonn had to say. Further books (*Gur Cake and Coal Blocks*; *The Labour and the Royal* and *Janey Mac, Me Shirt is Black*) followed, and I fondly remember his trips down memory lane on the radio in my youth, with his inimitable 'Dublin,

PUBLISHER'S FOREWORD BY IVAN O'BRIEN

my Dublin' signoff.

A twentieth-anniversary edition of the book was published in 1994, significantly updated to reflect the changes that the city had undergone in the interim, with more buildings let fall into ruin: but there were real improvements too. I know that Éamonn would be thrilled that his son Shane was able to drive the building of an important interpretive centre in Glasnevin Cemetery, and that he would approve of the long-overdue Croppies' Acre Memorial Garden. The renovation of Smithfield, while flawed, has brought new energy to that part of the city and there is a genuine pride in the city's beautiful Georgian heritage.

For this fiftieth anniversary edition, it was impossible to update the book in a meaningful way. So much has changed, with the docks now a vibrant technology hub, Temple Bar a party zone and the trams returned in the new guise as the LUAS light rail. Éamonn would mourn the passing of the Tivoli, but recognise every bit of the maze of streets behind Mother Redcaps, and be glad that Moore Street still has the energy of a vibrant street market.

This book is a celebration of a time that has passed, a time when the city was small enough for everybody to have met Bang Bang or seen Jimmy O'Dea performing with Maureen Potter. For The O'Brien Press it marks half a century of publishing Irish books for Irish people of all ages. With almost 2,500 books published, and more booksellers than ever throughout the country, we are determined that the legacy of Tom and Michael O'Brien, and Éamonn MacThomáis, is respected and built on.

So have yourself a read and let a master storyteller take you back to the childhood of a man who was born in Dublin nearly a century ago, in 1927.

Ivan O'Brien, 2024

The present church of St Nicholas of Myra in Francis Street.

FOREWORD BY DONAL FALLON

Before Éamonn MacThomáis, he was Edward Patrick Thomas.

Born in Rathmines in 1927, the man who would become Dublin's most familiar historian was the son of a chief fire officer in the Rathmines Fire Brigade. With its own fire service, town hall and local authorities, Rathmines was a township beyond the canals that defined a very different Dublin. Only a young boy when his father died, he would recall the family being moved on to Goldenbridge, and how:

> *The furniture van was gone and I remember standing in the hallway of the empty house with a small green vase in my hands. I noticed that the wallpaper was cleaner in those places which had been covered by pictures. At that moment the Rathmines Town Hall clock rang out and I nearly let the vase fall. It was the first and the last time I heard it strike.*

Like many in the Republican movement of his time, he would change his name to Irish, and it is the name of Éamonn MacThomáis that is remembered. Still, his life before historical research and Republican political activity helps us understand the paths he would take. As a young delivery boy working in the city, he came to know the city intimately, and to question its origins. He remembered delivering to Henrietta Street, and entering a tenement home to find that 'the banisters were broken in parts, and the paint was worn from the stairs. I later found out that ten families lived in each house that was broken down. The nice houses were doctors or solicitors or offices or convents... the broken houses were part of the slums of Dublin.'

Active in the Republican movement from the early 1950s, MacThomáis was part of the IRA's Border Campaign, which initially galvanised Republican feeling in the south, before fading out. It led to periods of imprisonment, an environment in which he would intellectually thrive, using time to research, write and lecture.

His first publication, released in October 1965 on the eve of the Golden Jubilee of the Rising, was *Down Dublin Streets: 1916*. It contained the classic formula of a MacThomáis text – it was as much about topography, and the streets of Dublin, as history. It sought to show the hidden histories of familiar places. It was unashamedly Republican. It was accessible. It was also a great success. It was published by The Irish Book Bureau, through Joe Clarke, a 1916 veteran. His second book *The Lady at the Gate* (named in honour of the republican women who held vigil outside prisons like Mountjoy and Kilmainham) was published by the same press in 1967.

When later imprisoned as a result of his editorship of *An Phoblacht*, the Republican newspaper, Mac Thomáis commenced work on this book, a work that led the *Irish Press* to insist 'only James Joyce and Flann O'Brien have caught the mood of Dublin as well as Eamonn MacThomáis.' When Éamonn was briefly granted parole to attend to a family matter, newspapers reported that the 'author of the current best-selling non-fiction book in the country, *Me Jewel and Darlin' Dublin*, is due to return to Portlaoise next Saturday morning.'

Dublin in the 1970s was a city some viewed as only fit for the wrecking ball, a time captured well in Frank McDonald's battle cry text *The Destruction of Dublin*. But here, amidst so much destruction, was a celebration of the Liberties, of Ringsend, of the backstreets and alleys. More than anything, it was a celebration of the working-class people of Dublin and their traditions.

In time, MacThomáis would also shine as a broadcaster, working with the brilliant team of David and Sally Shaw-Smith to produce *Dublin: A Personal View*. That this show has enjoyed a revival of interest in recent times, with clips trending on social media sites and even TikTok, is testament to the ability of such social history to transcend barriers of age or demographic.

Reflecting on how the city has changed in the fifty years since the first publication of this book, it's worth noting that MacThomáis was not only a Republican activist, but also a campaigner for the city. He provided a heartfelt introduction to Deirdre Kelly's *Hands Off Dublin*, a book produced by the Living City Group which made a passionate argument that the inner-city required people and communities to live within it. It was time, MacThomáis argued, to acknowledge that 'the destruction of Dublin has gone on too long, it's time to call a halt.' Several campaigns that MacThomáis was a supporter of succeeded in saving some of the historic fabric of the city.

MacThomais died in August 2002, at the age of seventy-five. He was survived by four children and his beloved wife Rosaleen. Newspaper headlines heralded him as the 'City's Champion' and the 'Quintessential Dubliner'. There was beautiful continuity in his son, Shane, pursuing a career as a historian, with the same commitment to a kind of history that was both thorough and accessible. Shane would remember Éamonn's funeral as a fine tribute, capturing what he meant to so many different Dubliners:

The gathering of people could be described as nothing short of eclectic. Every shade of politics was present, from the communist reds to the green ultra nationalists. But the divergences were not just in politics. Lollypop women stood beside Trinity professors, while balladeers and newsreaders looked at each other's shoes. It was at that point that I realised that a funeral was, in a way, a short biography of a person's life and that so much could be learned from one.

Donal Fallon, 2024

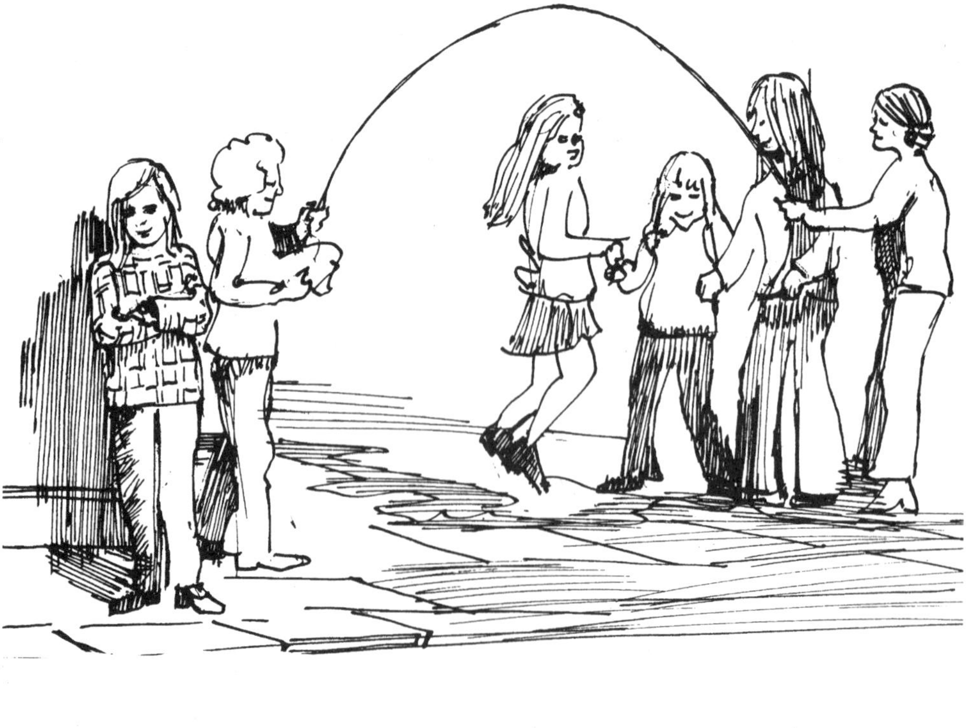

CHAPTER 1

A CHILD'S WORLD

THE FOURPENNY RUSH

First it was the Twopenny Rush, then the Threepenny Rush and, when they got the picture house painted and new wooderners and cushioners installed, it went up to the Fourpenny Rush.

My friend Bonker said that the price now was 'universal'.

'What does that mean?' we asked. 'All over the world,' said Bonker, 'it's fourpence everywhere. It's something to do with the union.' But we were never able to figure out what the South Dublin Union – St James's Hospital for the poor – had to do with the price of the pictures on a Saturday or Sunday afternoon.

The Fourpenny Rush in the local cinemas kept the kids off the streets. It taught them what they never learned in school. It was a college in memory training because every kid could tell you, line for line and act for act, all about the Big Picture or the Follier-Upper (serial picture).

An hour before the show started a queue would form. The ushers would beat the children back with leather belts. 'Keep in line, keep in line,' they shouted as the sweat rolled off their brows. It was quite an effort trying to handle a thousand children pushing and shoving, pulling pigtails, throwing orange peels and clutching dearly to the fourpence admission fee.

Bonker was right. It was fourpence everywhere as we toured the local cinemas of Dublin. They were: the 'Core' at Inchicore, the 'Ri' (Rialto) and the 'Leinster' at Dolphin's Barn, the 'Fountain' in James's Street, the 'Tivo' in Francis Street, the 'Mayro' in Mary Street, the 'Phoeno' on the quays and the 'Broad' or the 'Manor' in Manor Street. All these cinemas have since been closed, except for the 'Tivo' which is now the Tivoli Theatre, run by Tony Byrne.

Sometimes we went into town to the Pillar cinema or the Grand Central in O'Connell Street or around to the Masterpiece or the New Electric in Talbot Street. At other times, we would take our custom to the Camden or the 'Lux' (De-Luxe) in Camden Street or the Green in St Stephen's Green. Now and then we ventured out as far as the Stella and the 'Prinner' (Princess) on the Rathmines Road, nearly facing 'Homeville' where I was born. It was Shanks's mare there and back from our homes in Kilmainham. If we had a penny to spend, the last thing we'd spend it on was a tram or a bus. Wet or fine, we walked everywhere.

The hero in the picture was known as 'the Chap'. He always had a 'Pal' and a dog or a horse which could do tricks. They all got a roaring standing ovation, while the head crook and the other crooks all got a hiss and a boo. We hated love pictures. What we liked best were Gene Autry, Tom Mix, Roy Rogers, Buck Jones and Tarzan because they never kissed girls. No matter how tough the fight, Gene Autry never lost his hat – and he could kill twelve Indians with one shot out of his gun.

Best for laughs were Wheeler and Wolsey, Charlie Chaplin, the Keystone Cops, Pop-Eye and his girlfriend Olive Oyle and Laurel and Hardy ('This is another nice mess you've gotten me into, Stanley.') Although we hated girls, Shirley Temple was different and we all saw *The Little Princess* three times. Dublin had its own Shirley Temple contest and a little girl from the road where I lived was in the first ten.

The outstanding greats of those days were *Boys' Town* with Mickey Rooney and Spencer Tracey, the Dead End Kids in *Angels with Dirty Faces*, James Cagney and *The Roaring Twenties*, *The Bolero* with George Raft, *Northwest Passage*, *Mr Stanley and Dr Livingstone*, *Jesse James*, *The Daltons Ride Again*, and *Charlie Chan*. We also loved Peter Lorre in detective pictures, *Murder at the Wax Museum* and the wonderful singing pictures of Nelson Eddy and Jeanette McDonald.

The ice-skating queen, Sonja Heinie, starred in the film *One in a Million*. The nearest we ever got to an ice-rink was when the dog pond froze over in the winter. It was a far cry from Torville and Dean, though now there are skating rinks in Phibsborough and Dolphin's Barn.

The former Tivoli Cinema, Francis Street, later used as a theatre.

The local cinema was more than a picture house. It was a community centre, a place to kill a few hours, something to look forward to, a chance for your mother to wear her new hat, a university of conversation, because whoever saw the picture first would come home and tell the whole road about it.

Television nearly killed the local cinema – though now it seems to be making a come-back – and it is helping to kill conversation. Practically everyone now watches films on television, because everyone has a telly. But the local cinema was different. Each cinema had two, sometimes three, different shows per week. If you missed the picture on Monday, you made sure that you saw it on Tuesday or Wednesday. No matter how good the telly, it's not a night out for the woman or man of the house. Men and women, boys and girls, could see a three-hour show sitting on the wooreners for fourpence.

At one stage, several cinemas took jam-jars instead of cash. That happened in the Twopenny Rush days. If you handed in a threepenny bit, you might be stuck with two one-pound jam-jars for your change. Can you imagine sitting on the wooreners, trying to balance two jam-jars, peel your orange and keep your eye on the Chap and the crook or worry yourself sick in case Stanley might not be able to find Dr Livingstone in the jungle? As my friend would say: 'To think that he could find him in a jungle like that and we got lost on the way home from the Roxy last Sunday!' The Roxy later became the Rotunda and then the Ambassador.

I knew a man who could neither read nor write, yet never missed a picture at his local cinema. He was a gifted story-teller and had the greatest memory in all Kilmainham. One day I said to him: 'You are a remarkable man. I wonder what you would be to-day if you could read and write!' He laughed and said: 'I never missed the books and the pens and sure there's only bad news in the newspapers. I learned all I ever wanted to know at the Fourpenny Rush in the Tivo. And do you see them Pullman seats to-day at £2.50 a go? Sure, you can't balance a drink on them. They can't hold a candle to the wooderners in the old Fourpenny Rush.'

A DUBLIN PENNY

'DID YOU SEE HIM, MARY?' my mother would say. 'Did you see him, looking up into their faces for a penny?' Whenever we stopped to talk to people on the street, I was always accused and bashed for looking up into their faces for a penny.

A penny was a lot of money in those days. With it you could buy the evening newspaper, weigh yourself, take a tram ride from Inchicore to College Green or buy a dinner for a poor man at the Little Flower Hall in the Liberties. A penny would buy a small bottle of milk or a large bag of broken biscuits from the Kingdom Stores in James's Street, a quarter of a pound of fat rashers (for a coddle), 2 ozs. of Maggie Ryan (margarine), a penny pot of jam, a large slice of Miss Noone's gur cake (fruit cake) hot from the oven or two coffin nails (cigarettes) and a few matches.

It would also buy a small packet of Lyons tea, a ball of blue, a tin of polish, a packet of Drummer dye, a pair of boot-laces, a seat on the fancy toilet in the Metropole, which is now demolished, or a box of Beecham's Pills, which the David Allen billboards said were worth a guinea a box. Perhaps for your penny you would like a white clay pipe which you didn't have to pick up if it fell, a split loaf (cat's lick and all), a large turnip, four onions or a pint of paraffin oil for the Sacred Heart lamp.

One of the many types of pennies used in Dublin over the centuries – George IV Copper Penny of 1823.

For the same penny you could have

a half-a-stone of logs, a little coal or a hot buttered egg from the Monument Creamery. A really special treat was a penny ice-cream wafer in Coppolo's of Cuffe Street, which you'd still be sucking at Rialto Bridge. A variety of sweets was available for the same penny – 12 rainbow caramels, 32 aniseed balls, 16 Jembo balls, 2 Peggy's legs or 2 lucky bags. You might prefer a pear, an apple, an orange or two taffy apples, a fishing net or two black babies – they were a halfpenny each. I can remember being sent home from school to get the halfpenny for the black babies which I forgot to bring with me that morning. Despite all the money I gave to the nuns and masters, I never saw any results and was always bitterly disappointed that they never brought in my black babies.

A penny would take you into Mass on a Sunday by the back door (the front

A long line of pennies all used in Dublin: 1. Hiberno-Norse Silver Penny struck in Dublin around 1000 - 1010 A.D. 2. Edward I Silver Penny struck in Dublin 1280. 3. The once-familiar Victorian Bronze Penny. 4. The 'golden hen' Irish Penny commonly used until replaced by decimal coins.

door was threepence). It would light a candle, buy a holy picture or could be presented to the poor woman with the child in her arms, sitting outside the church door. There were three types of Dublin pennies – the black Victorian type, the brown Edwardian type and the 'golden hen' with a harp on the other side. When my uncle came to visit, he always gave me a brand new golden hen. With a bit of skill the new penny could be transformed into a half-crown and, if I got a chance, I would change it in Muldowney's pub.

A story is told of a Dublin man who saw a large bottle of Gold Label whiskey in a public-house. On it was a price-tag marked 'One Penny'. He ordered the bottle, but the publican explained that a mistake had been made: the price was really 'One Pound'. With that a policeman came into the pub, heard the story and told the publican: 'The law says you must sell the bottle for a penny.' The lucky man then left the shop with the bottle. A few days later, the policeman met the man in the street. He laughed and said: 'Be the hokey, I'll never forget the look on the publican's face when I told him he would have to give you the big bottle of whiskey for a penny.' The man laughed back and said: 'You should have seen the look on his face when I went back the next day for a penny on the empty bottle.'

STREET GAMES

'ALL IN, ALL IN, THE GAME IS BROKE UP. All in, all in, the game is broke up.' Someone wasn't playing the game (Re-lieve-eeo); at least he wasn't playing it according to the Rowserstown rule book. So the words rang out in the night, like the old town criers: 'All in, all in, the game is broke up.' You could hear it a half-a-mile away. It always seemed to come just as you had found a good hiding-place in the Robbers' Den or across the Camac river near the old mill.

After the 'All in' sound we would come back to the street-lamp near the steps to the high road. The flies and moths were playing their own chasing game around the bright glow of the old gas lamp. 'What is it now?' 'Who broke up the game? Tell me who it was and I'll burst him.' 'Let's play another game.' 'Let's go home.' 'Let's start a fire.' 'Let's box the fox in the seven orchards.' 'Let's go up to Goldenbridge and play "Mind the Thread".'

'You-a, you-a, all the gang! You-a, you-a, all the gang! Don't forget your hoops' (a bicycle wheel without spokes or tyre and a piece of stick to beat the hoop along). Within seconds, fourteen hoops would be belting up Rowserstown and down to Kilmainham cross-roads. There were no traffic lights in those days and, if you stopped to let a tram pass, you were chicken.

Now for 'Mind the Thread'. 'Who's going to be on it? OK, you two.' Two boys, one at each side of the path, would sit on the ground pretending to be holding a piece of thread between them. It was held about six inches off the ground. The game would start as a man or woman came walking up the path. As soon as they came quite near, one of the boys would start shouting: 'Mrs., Mrs., mind the thread'. The poor woman thinks there's a thread on the ground so she starts lifting her legs, jumping and dancing to avoid it. 'Ah Mrs., Mrs., don't Mrs.' – that really had her hopping and we all sitting on the far side of the road, holding our sides with the laughter. Of course, some people knew we had no thread and entered into the game for fun. I played it a thousand times and I never remember anyone getting cross or cranky. Some were even surprised they could hop so high. If they had a sour face coming to the thread, they usually had a smile and a laugh leaving it.

'Follow the Leader' was a dangerous game, particularly if you were at the end of the line. The leader started off and the rest had to follow in single file. Anything the leader did, the others behind had to do also – knocking on doors, ringing bells, rattling ash-bin lids. By the time the last few got to the door or ash-bin, the owner was on the scene and all those at the rear of the line ended up with a few clouts on the ear or a kick in the backside.

'Kick the Can' was another favourite. I think this was invented for those

A CHILD'S WORLD

who couldn't afford a football. The boy 'on it' stood by the can and we had to kick the can without the boy 'on it' touching us. A lot of skill was required because some boys nearly sat on the can – nevertheless the can was often kicked up and down the road. The game usually ended with a good chase from Mr Kearney, who always threatened to get the po-liss. Poor Mr Kearney, he never had a dull evening.

We used to play another game called 'Rope the Door'. We would tie a rope to the door-knob and pull hard, then someone would knock on the door. Inside, poor Mr Kearney would be trying to open the door *in* and, at the same time, we would pull the door *out*. The tug-o'-war would go on for about five minutes. Then Mr Kearney would slip out the back-door wearing a pair of white runners and the Goldenbridge Steeplechase would begin. In later years, Mr Kearney told me that while he was mad with rage at the start of the chase, he was always in great form at the end of it. He was surprised that he could run so fast – he often caught a few of us – and it also helped to keep his weight down.

Whips and wooden tops, Taw in the Hole (marbles played like golf), Kattie, Combo Round Towers, Hide and Seek, Tip and Tig, Blind Man's Buff, hurling and football were all played on the road until you heard 'L.O.B., L.O.B. – Look out, boys, it's the cops.' Some children called them police, others called them cops, peelers, rawsers, or po-liss. The local sergeant often arrived on his upstairs model of a bicycle with its weak carbide lamp. The L.O.B. rarely failed. Even if it did, there was always plenty of time to get away. The sergeant took about ten minutes to get down off his bicycle, take the bicycle clips off his trousers and put out his carbide lamp before producing his notebook and pencil.

Card-playing was another favourite – rummy, pontoon, 15s, 25s, Snap, Old Maid, Dawn and Solo. Of these, Dawn was the most popular. It was played like this. The nine of trumps was known as Big Fat and the five of trumps as Little Fat. You played it with partners like whist. If you wanted your partner to lead with a certain suit of cards, you would work the tip-off system: Spades – 'I saw your father digging the garden to-day'; Diamonds – 'Mary Murphy's getting married. Her fella gave her a lovely ring'; Clubs – start singing 'The dear little shamrock, The sweet little shamrock'; Hearts – Put your hand on your chest and say: 'I've got an awful pain there'. Pretty primitive stuff, but it's surprising how it worked.

My favourite game was pitch and toss or 'Up to the Mottie', which was another form of it. Morning, noon and night I would play pitch and toss. I really loved it, until the man next door told my mother that he saw me playing it and that it was a very common game, as common as ditch-water, he said (a terrible insult) and she should make me give it up. A common game? If I'd known that night what I know now! Far from being a common game, it was in fact a royal game. It was started by King Edward III and the piece of stick on which you balanced the two coins got its name from him. They say he got very angry when he lost and used to throw down the tossing stick and say 'Feck it, feck it'. Thereafter the tossing stick has become known as the 'feck'. You put the two halfpennies on to the feck and toss them into the air – heads you win; harps or tails you lose.

An American visitor once said that the Dublin people were the holiest people in the world. 'How come?' asked his friend. 'Well,' said the American, 'at every street corner in Dublin the men stand around in circles, look up to Heaven, bow down their heads to the ground and shout out: "Good Christ, show us a head this time".' Pitch and toss was not only a child's game but was, and still is, a man's game. At the big pitch and toss school in the Brickfields I saw a man lose all his money and also his pony and trap. He had to go home on the crossbar of a friend's bicycle.

'Up to the Mottie' was another game. Our mottie was a small square piece of white broken delft stuck into the black clay on the side-path. When the

A CHILD'S WORLD

Corpo (Dublin Corporation) put concrete over this clay patch, we changed the game to 'Up to the Wall'. You needed only a halfpenny to enter the game. Each player pitched his halfpenny to the path wall, the nearest to the wall being the winner. He also got the first chance to toss the halfpenny for the next round.

After every wedding, well *almost* every wedding, in our local church, the groom or best man would 'grush the money'. As the newly-weds were about to drive off, the shouts went up: 'Mister, Mister, grush the money, grush the money' and a paper bag of pennies, halfpennies, threepenny bits and a few odd sixpence pieces would sail into the air and crash down in all directions, jingling and rolling. If you were lucky, you'd get a few pence or maybe a sixpenny piece. If you were unlucky, you'd get a kick on the ear and a black eye. The wedding of the year was judged by the size of the grush. With a penny grush-money and a lucky game of pitch and toss, you would have the price of the pictures and a few pence to spend or could take part in another game of pitch and toss the following day.

Sometimes we played the girls' games of skipping, swinging on a rope tied to a lamp-post or 'Piggy Beds' and 'Shop'. We always backed out when the games changed to 'School' or 'House' (mammies and daddies). 'Piggy Beds' was played on the paths with square or round rings marked out with chalk. The beds were like a ladder and you tipped the piggy (a shoe-polish box filled with clay) and it slid from bed to bed. If it went into the wrong bed or onto the chalk line of the bed you were out of the game. As you tipped the piggy with one foot, you hopped along at the same time. This really was a game of skill as you had to balance on one foot, tip the piggy with it and hop from bed to bed.

'Shop' was played with 'chaney money'. Chanies were pieces of broken delft, about the size of a new halfpenny. The more colourful the piece of chaney, the better it was as you could buy more with a few coloured pieces than you could with white ones. The contents of the 'shop' consisted of 'dog' or dock leaves (very good for cooling your hand if you got the sting of a nettle). Dandelion leaves were also for sale. We dried them in the sun, allowed them to rot and used them in clay pipes for tobacco. Other items were empty boxes, an odd jam-jar, comics and cigarette cards.

At that time cigarette cards were all the rage. They came free with every packet of cigarettes and were very colourful and educational. They came in series and a full set could be exchanged for gifts. Wills' 'Gold Flake' gave little playing cards and Carrolls gave 'Sweet Afton' coupons. For hours we would stand at Kilmainham Cross or at Sarah Bridge: 'Mister, any cigarette pictures, please?' Our pockets would be bulging with all sorts of cards. We never got any gifts for them but we got hours of pleasure. We swopped them for comics, sweets, a cigarette butt, a look at your Mickey Mouse watch. 'A go on a gig' cost 50 cigarette cards. The 'gig' was a flat board on four ball races (wheels) with a piece of strong twine for steering tied to the front axle. As you sat on the gig, your pal pushed your back; going down hills, it was all free-wheel.

We must not forget 'Cowboys and Indians' and 'Cops and Robbers'. They are both still favourites today. Strange how everyone wanted to be a robber. Another game, one I hated yet played because I didn't want to be chicken, was announced with the cry: 'Come on, will ya; come on, will ya. We're going to have a look at the stiffs.' Down to the Union Morgue we would go and in around the slabs where sixteen or seventeen bodies were awaiting burial. Some of them had pennies on their eyes and flies and bluebottles in their hundreds would be flying around like jet aeroplanes, landing now and again on the face of a corpse. I'd be shaking like a leaf as we crept around the bodies, the silence broken only by the buzzing of bluebottles. Then someone would shout out 'He moved, he moved' and without waiting to find out who had moved we would scatter for the door and not even Mick the Miller, the famous greyhound, could catch us.

CHAPTER 2

THE OLD WAYS

THE PAWNSHOPS OF DUBLIN

THE EARLY MONDAY MORNING TRAM was crowded. It was the same every Monday morning, not a seat or space to spare. Packed like a tin of sardines, the luggage bay was full of clothes, suits, blankets, shoes and a set of aluminium saucepans. Downstairs one woman sat beside St Joseph; another woman had the Child of Prague on her lap. Two eight-day clocks, each with a different time, took up two other seats. Upstairs, as usual, the Sacred Heart was in the front seat with a glass shade around him. He stood three feet tall, beside a big fat woman who had one arm on the seat and the other around the Sacred Heart.

When the tram stopped at The Fountain in James's Street, nearly everyone got off. First came the saucepans and the clothes, then St Joseph. Someone stood back to let the woman with the 'Child' descend. The last to leave was the Sacred Heart, followed by the two clocks. The procession crossed the street. At the sign of the three brass balls and the name Patrick Gorman, 31 James's Street, Pawnbroker, the procession ended as it moved up the lane to the counter door. The inside of the shop was a hive of activity. 'Ask for six and take four'; 'Wan gent's suit, navy blue, eight shillings'; 'Set of saucepans, three shillings'; 'The coat pocket is torn, Ma'am'; 'St Joseph again, four shillings'; 'The Child again, two-and-six'. 'Here's yer ticket ... yer ticket ... are ye deaf?'

'Give us six, Tom, on the coat, it's a Crombie'; 'I'll give ya four, the pocket is torn'; 'Ah go on, Tom, six shillings'; 'Four is all it's worth'; 'Well, give us five'; 'Four-and-six is as far as I go'; 'You're terrible mean, Tom. Make it five shillings'; 'Seven and sixpence the Sacred Heart in a glass shade'; 'Four-and-six for the coat. Here's your ticket'; 'Only four-and-six for a Crombie, I'll be kilt when I go home.'

The sign of the three brass balls is almost a thing of the past. In 1838 there were 700 pawnshops in Ireland and fifty-seven in Dublin. One hundred years later there were still forty or more in Dublin. There were three pawnshops in Summerhill, two in Gardiner Street, and one each of the following northside streets: Amiens Street, Talbot Street, Parnell Street, Granby Row, Capel Street, Ellis Quay, Queen Street, Dominick Street, Dorset Street and two in Marlborough Street.

On the south side of the Liffey, there were two in Cuffe Street and Charlemont Mall and one each in St James's Street, Bishop Street, Richmond Street, Bride Street, Clanbrassil Street, Francis Street, the Coombe, Ardee Street and Winetavern Street. Others were located in Fleet Street, Erne Street, Lombard Street, Baggot Street, Mount Street, Ringsend, at 19½ Main Street, Blackrock, and two in Lower George's Street, Dun Laoghaire. All were under private names with the exception of the one in 7 Buckingham Street, which was registered as 'The Great Northern Pawn Office'.

The first things people pawned were their own clothes – coats, dresses, suits, hats, etc. As they got poorer, they pawned the clothes off the bed. As they got poorer still, they pawned religious pictures, statues, clocks, pots, pans, patriotic pictures. And when they were the poorest of the poor they pawned the chair they sat on. The pawnbroker did not make money on the objects pawned, even if the objects were never redeemed. He made his money on the number of pledges (items pawned). The pawnbroker had a fixed levy on each pawn ticket and because of the thousands of tickets issued the profits

THE OLD WAYS

John Brereton's of Capel Street, with the familiar sign.

rolled in. The pawn office was open from early morning until 10.30 p.m. Monday to Saturday. The pawnbroker's tickets stated: 'Fine Airy Wardrobes for your Clothes.' The fine airy wardrobes were dozens of six-inch nails stuck into a wooden wall.

Some people didn't give a damn being seen going to the pawn. Others tried to slip in and out unnoticed. From Trinity College students came with camel-hair coats, college books, Boswell's *The Life of Samuel Johnson*, *Gulliver's Travels*, gold watches and straw hats. Others came with saucepans with no lids, broken shoes, torn coats, religious statues, ponies and carts, bicycles, suites of furniture and gold wedding rings. The pawn was the place to go, make your pledge, get your ticket, redeem the article the next Saturday and pledge it back in the following Monday. Year in, year out, the pawn was a

ME JEWEL AND DARLIN' DUBLIN

Some auction advertisements from Dublin pawnbrokers.

way of life. It put bread on many a poor man's table and saved many a college student from being evicted out of his Rathmines flat.

The Pawnbrokers' Assistants were a very respectable class of gentlemen. At one time they had to live in and were not allowed to get married until they served their seven years' apprenticeship. Many got married before the allowed time and had to go to bed with their wives during their dinner hour. I knew one assistant who changed his clothes every day. He had to: his mother wouldn't let him in otherwise. 'Take off your flea suit before you come in here,' she'd say, as she threw another suit out the kitchen window. Poor John – he's dead now – used to change in a shed in the back garden.

Tommy Armstrong was another character who had a pawnshop in Ardee Street. He always tied his trousers at the knees to keep the fleas out. Around this time, Singer sewing-machines were being sold door-to-door at a shilling per week. One day a man stuck his head into Tommy's pawnshop and said:

'Mister A, Mister A, would you be interested in a Singer sewing-machine?' ''Deed and I wouldn't,' said Tommy. 'Sure every arsehole in Dublin has wan of them.' Tommy followed a long line of tradition in the pawnbroking business.

If a rich man wanted money he took the deeds of his house or land to the bank and arranged a loan. That was a business transaction and he was a business-man. If a poor woman wanted bread for her children she took the clothes off the bed, went to the pawn, made a pledge and she was a pauper.

St Nicholas of Myra Church in Francis Street has a nice statue of the saint with three gold balls, representing him as the Giver of Gifts. The Lombards may have started the tradition. They were merchants, goldsmiths and mon-

One of the many old pawnbrokers who have since closed the door, Weafer's of Dorset Street.

ey-lenders who came from Genoa, Florence and Vienna. First, they had three gold plates as their symbol. Later, the three gold plates were replaced by three gold balls. The Lombards gave us many of the commercial terms which we use every day: debtor, creditor, cash, bank, journal, diary, ditto, and the old £. s. d. which originally stood for Libri, Soldi and Denarii. The Lombards granted the first loan to the States and took the customs duties (from imports) as their pledges.

The first pawnshop was set up in Rome by the Emperor Augustus. When he fed people to the lions in the Coliseum he took over their property and used it to grant small loans. In the fifteenth century, a Franciscan priest set up a pawnshop in Assisi. His was a special type known as the House of Mont-de-Piete. Germany and Italy followed suit and King Billy (William of Orange) organised one in Holland.

The oldest pawn record in the National Library is a letter to Col. J. Fitzsimmons, Roscommon, dated February 1664, concerning the redeeming of the waistcoat of Sir James Dillon which was pawned for £10 by Lady Dillon. In 1634 the Dublin Corporation pawned the City Seal for £1,000.

'Ask for six and take four,' and 'I don't care if you're kilt,' were common instructions. Today pawnbroking continues and so do the pawn office auction sales. You'll see them advertised in the small ad. columns of the evening papers. The next time you see three brass balls you'll know the sign doesn't mean 'Two to wan, you won't get it back.'

DUBLIN PAWNSHOP

Three brass balls
    Four black shawls
    A clock, St Anthony,
    Robert Emmet,
    A willow delft,
    Another shawl
    With bedclothes.
    A man with two suits
    Scholars with University books.
    A plumber with a bicycle,
    A jarvey with no horse –
    All pledged and lodged
    For bread, rent
    And drink.
    'One-and-nine
    That's it,'
    'Give us two bob,
    He'll have a fit,'
    'One-and-nine
    It's a torn quilt,'
    'The devil take ya
    I'll be kilt,'
    'Mind the clock –
    Don't kick it
    Go home!
    There's your ticket.'
    Tenement clothes
    Stored on shelf.
    Emmet and Anthony
    With willow delft,
    One of the books
    The life of Tone
    With eight-day clock.

On its own
And stable
Paddy Murphy's roan.
Scholars and shawls
Move away
Surviving for another day.
Will he miss
Young Emmet
At his tay?
God love us all,
Sure we have to pay –
He knows
We've got no other way.
And Emmet won't mind
Another stay
At his uncle Jemmy's.
Éamonn Mac Thomáis.

THE COMEDY KING

'I TOLD YOU,' MY MOTHER SAID. 'How many more times are you going to ask me? His name is Jimmy O'Dea and he comes from a very comfortable family. His father spent pounds on his education and he was wild when Jimmy gave up his profession to go on the stage.' Later on that night my mother told me that the first time she saw him on stage he was like a little prince. She described his clothes down to the last detail – his suit, hat, shirt and the shine on his shoes. 'Oh,' she said, 'he was like a little prince, as if he had just stepped out of a hat box.'

I was ten years of age and had just returned home from my first visit to the Gaiety Theatre and the Jimmy O'Dea pantomime. For many days after, my mind was filled with memories of the Gaiety, the climb up the stairs to the gallery, the wooden step-like seats, the music, the coloured lights, the white spot-light, the safety curtain which I read at least a dozen times, the smell of oranges and the funny little man named Jimmy O'Dea. That day my hands were sore from clapping so I copied the people beside me and banged my 'Little Duke' boots on the gallery floor. A prince, my mother called him. Well, to me he was another King of Dublin, a king who made people laugh and sing. He made people happy and at times laughed himself, as the curtain kept rising and falling.

Jimmy O'Dea was a legend in his own lifetime and as I grew into my teens I seldom missed any of his shows. He was

Jimmy O'Dea.

a master of comedy and left a million memories to audiences from the provinces, Dublin and overseas. Like all the great troupers, his name was always linked with shows for the poor and deserving causes.

Harry O'Donovan, another great name in Dublin's theatreland, wrote the scripts and Jimmy brought the characters to life. Together they created 'Biddy Mulligan, the pride of the Coombe', which was Jimmy's favourite role. It happened this way. One evening, as Jimmy and Harry were walking down Henry Street, Harry said: 'Jimmy, we must get you a particular type of character, something or someone that you will be recognised as. Chaplin has his Derby hat and walking stick.' Just at that moment a woman came out of a public-house in Moore Street, shouting at a man behind her: 'Go along outa that, you bowsie.' O'Donovan's eyes twinkled, his mind flashed, his fingers clicked and O'Dea soon got the message. 'That's it,' said Harry, 'a woman of Dublin talking like that woman,' and so 'Biddy' was born in the heart of Moore Street. Although Harry wrote many scripts on Moore Street, he made 'Biddy' a lady of the Liberties, who lived in the Coombe and sold her wares

Jimmy O'Dea and Maureen Potter.

at Patrick Street corner.

Jimmy O'Dea was born in April 1899 at 11 Lower Bridge Street. His parents, James and Martha O'Dea, were both comfortable business people. His house was three doors from where Oliver Bond lived and across the road from the Old Brazen Head Inn. Next door, No. 12, was Mullett's public-house. When Jimmy was seven years of age, his aunt showed him the window in Mullett's where the true green flag of Ireland was displayed while all Dublin was decked out in red, white and blue.

Jimmy was born a few paces from the old Ford of Hurdles. He was baptised in St Audoen's parish church in High Street. In his youth he served as an altar boy in the Augustinian Church, John's Lane. A good education and a good profession was planned by Jimmy's father. His first school-days were spent at the Holy Faith preparatory school at Kilcoole, Co. Wicklow. From here he went to the Marist Fathers in Dundalk, then to the Jesuits in Belvedere College and finally to the Holy Ghost Fathers at Blackrock College.

It was decided that Jimmy would become an optician and he was apprenticed to Mr John Murray of 1 Duke Street. Murray was a leading ophthalmic optician with branch offices at 52 Queen Street, Glasgow, and 100 Lothian Street, Edinburgh. He was also Hon. Secretary of the Irish Optical Association. In a few years, Jimmy qualified and opened his own practice in South Frederick Street, Dublin. That was in 1921. Six years later he left his optician's practice in the care of his sister, Rita, also an optician, to become a professional artist.

Jimmy's early gramophone records are still in many Dublin homes and I can remember well, after my first visit to the Gaiety, volunteering every Sunday night to turn the handle of the old-style His Master's Voice-type gramophone to hear Jimmy O'Dea singing about 'The Charladies' Ball' or 'Putting his Sixpence each way on Water Sprite'.

THE CHARLADIES' BALL

You may talk of your outings, your picnics and parties
Your dinners and dances and hoolies and all
But wait till I tell ya the gas that we had
When we went to the Charladies' fancy-dress ball.

I was there as Queen Anne and I went with me man
He was dressed as a monkey locked up in a cage
We had pierettes and pierrots and hockeytops and whatnots
And stars that you'd see on the talkies and stage.

CHORUS
At the Charladies' Ball people said one and all

ME JEWEL AND DARLIN' DUBLIN

You're the belle of the ball, Mrs Mulligan
We had one-steps and two-steps and the divil knows what new steps
We swore that we'd never be done again, bedad.
We had wine, Guinness and Jameson
We had cocktails and cocoa and all.
We had champagne that night but we'd real pain next morning
The night that we danced at the Charladies' Ball.

There were injuns and cowboys that came from Drumcondra
We had Francis Street fairies, all diamonds and stars
There was one of the Rooney's like the clock over Mooney's
And a telegraph boy as a message from Mars.

Mary Moore from the Lotts was the Queen of the Scots
With a crown out'a Woolworth's perched up on her dome
There was young Jimmy Whitehouse dressed up as a lighthouse
And a Camden Street Garbo that should've gone home.

CHORUS
At the Charladies' Ball people said one and all
You're the belle of the ball, Mrs Mulligan
We had one-steps and two-steps and the divil knows what new steps
We swore that we'd never be done again, bedad.
We had wine, porter and Jameson
We had cocktails and cocoa and all
We had rumbas and tangos, half-sets and fandangoes
That night that we danced at the Charladies' Ball.

Mary Ellen O'Rourke was the Queen of the Dawn
By 1.30 she looked like a rale dirty night
Mickey Farren the betser was dressed as a jester
He burst his balloon and dropped dead with the fright.

Jim Barr went as Bovril, stops that sinkin' feelin'
Astride of a bottle, pyjamas and all

He bumped into Faust who was gloriously soused
And the two of them were sunk at the end of the hall.

CHORUS
At the Charladies' Ball people said one and all
You're the belle of the ball Mrs Mulligan
We had one-steps and two-steps and the divil knows what new steps
We swore that we'd never be done again bedad.
We had wine, porter and Jameson
We had cocktails and cocoa and all
We'd a nice sit-down tea, but we fell down to supper
The night that we danced at the Charladies' Ball.

Jimmy O'Dea was at home in front of the footlights and yet I heard him say that, every time the curtain went up, he got butterflies in his stomach. He loved people and was always happiest when he was in front of them on the stage, giving them his best in entertainment.

It's true to say that Dublin's great trouper, Maureen Potter, got part of her greatness from Jimmy O'Dea. When they acted together they were the King and Queen of Dublin's comedy. Nevertheless, the name O'Dea must always be linked with the name O'Donovan. For close on forty years they were the leaders of Dublin's wit and comedy. When both died, part of Dublin died with them. The name and the memory of O'Dea and O'Donovan will always have a special place in the hearts of all Dubliners.

The next time you go down Moore Street, listen for the real Biddy Mulligan: 'It's the likes of me that has the likes of you driving around in your Rollses-Royces.' You might even see the twinkle in Harry O'Donovan's eyes or the smile on Jimmy O'Dea's lips.

> **Gaiety Theatre**
> SOUTH KING STREET, DUBLIN
> Telegrams: "GAIETY," DUBLIN.   Telephone 78205/6
> Proprietors: THE GAIETY THEATRE (DUBLIN) LTD.
> Resident Manager: PHIL O'KELLY
>
> **Commencing July 25th, 1960**
> NIGHTLY 8 P.M.   MATINEE: SATURDAY 2.30 P.M.
>
> O'D PRODUCTIONS present
>
> ## JIMMY O'DEA
> IN
> # Flights of Fancy
> A Topical Revue by HARRY O'DONOVAN
> with
> DANNY CUMMINS   MARIE CONMEE   VERNON HAYDEN
> FRANK O'DONOVAN   NOEL & URSULA DOYLE   SHELAGH DEY
> EDMOND BROWNE   PATRICIA O'KEEFFE   DERRY O'DONOVAN
> EDDIE WARD-MILLS   JAMES KENT
>
> —— SPECIAL GUEST ARTISTES ——
> ALBERT LE BAS   3 DOMINOES
> DONOVAN & HAYES   ALEX MATISON
>
> THE GAIETY GIRLS   THE GAIETY MALE DANCERS
>
> **Produced by JIMMY O'DEA**
>
> Asst. Producer: RONNIE WALSH   Choreography by SHELAGH DEY
> Musical Director: LESLIE BERESFORD
> Scenery designed and painted by ROBERT HEADE
> Dancers oy permission of the Desmond Domican Academy.
>
> BEFORE AND AFTER THE SHOW AND AT THE INTERVAL MEET YOUR FRIENDS IN THE LOUNGE BARS. TABLES MAY BE RESERVED IN THE TEA ROOMS.
>
> The public may leave at the end of the performance by all exit doors. Person shall not be permitted to stand or sit in any of the gangways intersecting the seating, or to sit in any of the other gangways.—Copy Bye-Law.

A playbill.

STREET CHARACTERS

'BANG BANG', THE FAMOUS CHARACTER of the Liberties, was an impostor. Yes, I was shocked! I could not believe my ears, but he told me so himself, straight from Bang Bang's lips. He was a foreigner, born in the Rotunda Hospital on the north side of Dublin. He has now passed away.

And remember what my grandmother used to say: 'If you have to cross

THE OLD WAYS

Church Street Bridge to go home, you're a bloody foreigner, and you'll need a passport to re-enter the Liberties of Dublin.' Well, 'Bang Bang' showed me his 'passport', his pension-book, from which I jotted down the details: Thomas Dudley, 50b Bridgefoot Street, Dublin. No mention of the words 'Bang Bang'. He told me he'd rather be called Lord Dudley. 'I had no mammy or daddy,' he said. 'The nuns in Cabra reared me. I was born in the Rotunda. I had another mammy in Hill Street. I also lived in Newmarket ... your hand is lovely and warm sir, you're a gentleman, sir. Ye know me, don't ye, sir? I'm going blind,' he added. 'My eyes are very bad. I don't like where I'm living. I want to go back to the old place. Do you mind me holding your hand, sir? Lord Dudley, sir, why don't they call me Lord Dudley?' 'Bang Bang, Lord Dudley,' I said. 'It's an honour to meet you again after all these years.' 'And me too, sir. Look sir, look sir, I still have it, sir.'

He let go my hand and from his inside coat pocket he drew his gun – a long door-key, worn thin and shining from constant use down the years as he bang-banged with it all over Dublin and the Liberties. 'I don't use it much now,' he said, 'not since I became Lord Dudley. I only use it an odd time. BANG BANG,' he said in farewell, 'YOU'RE DEAD.'

Whenever 'Bang Bang' was on a bus or tram they were vehicles of happiness. He made the people laugh. He helped them to forget their worries as he played cowboys and Indians with them in the streets of Dublin. Many Dublin people were seen dodging in and out of doorways and falling dead in the streets as they tried to shoot 'Bang Bang'.

I met him in Thomas Street in 1973 during the Liberties Festival so I took him to the traditional concert of Irish music in St Catherine's. There I introduced him to the audience. True to his name and tradition, he took out his door-key and proclaimed: 'BANG BANG, BANG BANG. YOU'RE DEAD!' The audience gave him a wonderful reception and you could see their faces brighten and light up with smiles. Outside the door, he said: 'Thank you, sir, for bringing me in, sir. They all know me, sir. They like me too. It's a lovely church, sir. It's the first time I was ever in it – and they liked me, sir.' 'Bang Bang, Lord Dudley,' I said, 'not only do they like you – they love you and whenever they write the history of the Liberties it won't be complete unless it mentions your name.' He smiled, yet his eyes were sad and weak. He smiled again and half-said to himself: 'They like me, they like me, sir.' I gave him a few bob for a jar or two and promised to look him up again for a chat.

He held my hand in an iron grip for twenty minutes and again went over his life story. 'You know where I live now, sir. Call anytime. Just ask for Lord Dudley, sir.' He let go my hand and stood at the door of Ryan's public house, looking after me until I turned the corner at John's Lane and was out of sight.

♥ ♥ ♥

Dan Donnelly of Bull Alley became the champion boxer of the world when he defeated Cooper, an Englishman, in Donnelly's Hollow on the plains of the Curragh in Co. Kildare. The sugar-cane man, who lived in the Spitalfields

Dan Donnelly – Champion boxer of the World.

THE OLD WAYS

and who sold sweet bars, told the story of the first fight over and over again. He said Donnelly was in trouble in the seventh round and was nearly beaten but he managed to throw a few sweet bars into Donnelly's gob and the rest of the story is history.

Donnelly returned to Dublin leading a victory parade. Thousands marched while thousands of others lined the pavements, cheering and singing. Donnelly was in an open carriage drawn by four white horses. His mother, a big fat woman, sat beside him. When the parade reached James's Street (it took seventeen days to come from the Curragh with a stop at every public-house) his mother stripped down to the waist. Slapping her bosom now and again, she cried out: 'I'm the woman who reared him and these are the breasts that fed him.' When the parade reached the Coombe, they all adjourned to the Four Corners of Hell for drinks all round. Another fight nearly started between the mother and the sugar-cane man, as they both claimed it was their product which gave Dan the strength for the final knock-out blow.

♥ ♥ ♥

'The Bird' Flanagan got his name from the time he went to a fancy-dress ball dressed as a bird. When he didn't win a prize, he went up onto the stage where the judge sat, laid an egg and then threw it at the judge. 'The Bird' was a wealthy man and owned cabbage-fields all over Crumlin, Drimnagh and Walkinstown. These lands at one time belonged to a man named Keogh, who was a member of the Invincibles and escaped with his family to America after Cavendish and Burke were killed in the Phoenix Park.

♥ ♥ ♥

'Endymion' was a character who haunted Grafton Street and College Green. He dressed in a deerstalker hat, knee breeches, tunic shirt and buckled shoes. He always carried a few spare swords, a fishing rod and an umbrella which was always up on a fine day and down on a wet day. Sometimes he fished through the railings of Trinity College.

'Endymion' lived in Pleasant Street. He used a compass to find his way home from O'Connell Street daily and he gave a sword salute to the Ballast Office clock. He would then set his alarm clock by it, wet his finger, hold it up to see which way the wind was blowing, take out his compass, get his bearing and make for home. The compass never let him down – even when he went home via James's Street, Kilmainham, South Circular Road, Rialto Bridge and Heytesbury Street.

♥ ♥ ♥

Endymion, complete with sword and umbrella.

The blind ballad singer, Michael Moran, better known as Zozimus.

'Zozimus', Michael Moran, the blind ballad singer, was born in Faddle Alley in 1794. He lost the sight of both eyes two weeks after birth. It's a miracle how he was able to learn so many ballads and poems and he must have had a brilliant memory. He lived all his life in the Liberties and ended his days in 14½ Patrick Street.

His friends were other street characters of the period known as 'Owny the Fool', who was as wise as an owl, 'Peg the Man', 'Fat Mary', the prima donna of the Dublin streets, 'Stoney Pockets', 'The Dear Man' and several others who performed on the streets of Dublin.

'Zozimus' got his name from the poem of St Mary of Egypt written by Bishop Coyle, the name being mentioned many times in the poem. His only trips outside the Liberties were to Cullenswood in Ranelagh, where he entertained at the runaway marriages which were performed by a German clergyman named Schultz. The journeys were usually made on Bobby Tomkins's horse and dray, that is whenever the dray wasn't in the pawn-office yard.

'Zozimus' died on 3 April 1846, and was buried in Glasnevin Cemetery. His grave is No. AG-30. Fr Nicholas O'Keefe, a curate of Francis Street church who later became P.P. Rush, attended him in his last illness. The day he died, 'Zozimus' said: 'Excuse me, your Riverence, I won't be a minute, I'm dictating me funeral arrangements.' 'Zozimus' had a great fear that the sack-'em-ups would get him and his corpse would end up in the College of Surgeons.

A week after he died, a miniature painter named Horatio Nelson of Grafton Street produced a painting of 'Zozimus, Rhymer and Reciter.' A short time after this, a man appeared in Patrick Street dressed like him and claimed he was the real 'Zozimus'. He went from pub to pub claiming his free whiskey droppings (the whiskey which spilled into a tray while it was being poured out). 'Stoney Pockets', another well-known character, said it was a bloody good job they put 'Zozimus' down a hole in Glasnevin because, if the sack-'em-ups had got him to the College of Surgeons, whiskey would have been banned for ever.

♥ ♥ ♥

'President Keely' was another Dublin character. 'The ship can't go out if it doesn't come in. The sun will never fall in Dublin; it will do as I say. Vote Number One, President Keely. The Ministers use only silver keys but President Keely uses gold keys.' During the presidential elections, Keely was a very busy man and he always appeared on the day of the inauguration ceremony. He would march up Lord Edward Street pushing a handcart, wearing a tall silk hat with his name 'Keely' written on it. He always got a better ovation than the President-elect.

♥ ♥ ♥

THE OLD WAYS

'Tie-Me-Up' was another character who provided great entertainment. I never knew his real name but he always stood at the Metal Bridge, stripped to the waist, cracking a big whip and shouting: 'Tie me up, Tie me up.' He would get a few men to tie him in chains and then put a strait-jacket on him. He'd twist, turn, roll over, twist again and his eyes would nearly burst out of his head. He'd roar with pain and then after about twelve minutes he would free himself to the applause of the audience. The hat would then go around. For an encore he would balance a heavy cart-wheel on his chin or lie on broken glass.

♥ ♥ ♥

'Specs' was another widely-known character and again I have not uncovered his real name. He lived somewhere in Crumlin. He was over six feet tall and always had a piece of cloth tied from the front wheel to the handlebars of his bike to catch the wind and carry him along like a sailing boat. He could peel an apple without breaking the skin and when he finished his work of art he would throw away the apple and eat the skin.

One day he asked us to put wind in his sails, so we took it he wanted the wheels of his bike pumped. This happened during the last war when cigarettes were very scarce. When we finished the job, he took a blue tin box, which usually contained 100 Player's cigarettes, from his saddle bag. Our eyes nearly popped out of our heads. He said: 'You are very good lads and I'm going to give you three each.' 'Specs' then opened the box and gave each of us three conversation lozenges – 'You're Cute', 'Kiss Me', 'Lover Boy', etc. Well, you should have heard our conversation about 'Specs', his boat-bike and his sweets. One thing I'm sure of, it will never get into print or onto conversation lozenges.

♥ ♥ ♥

'Lino' was another character. He got his name because he was always lying on the floor. He was another 'Bang Bang' type who brought happiness and joy into people's lives every day.

A lovely man, a darlin' man, me oul' flower, Lino, more power to your elbow.

❤ ❤ ❤

And we must remember Matt Talbot, loved by the poor. Dublin's holy man, he slept on planks of wood and wore chains around his body. He died on his way to Mass in Granby Lane. Many times I heard my mother say: 'Don't worry, Mary. I'll get a job. Matt Talbot won't let me down.' Later in the day word would come to my mother. 'Yes, you are to start tomorrow morning at eight. I think it's a few months' work.' 'I told you, Mary,' my mother would say. 'Matt never let me down yet. He knows what it's like to be idle in Dublin and he always looks after his own.' A few pennies would then go into St Anthony's Box (bread for the poor) and my mother would say: 'I'm giving it to you, Anthony, but I know it was Matt the Dubliner who got me the job.'

❤ ❤ ❤

Siki, 'Cyclone' Warren, was a negro boxer who came to Dublin, fell in love with the city and its people and never left. He was a big man with big feet and was very popular with Dubliners. At one time he was used to advertise Nugget boot polish. He used to stand on a piece of black wood that looked like black marble. Written on it were the words 'Nugget Polish'. He was truly a very likeable character.

❤ ❤ ❤

'Billy in the Bowl' (Billy Davis) was born without legs and he used to sit in an iron bowl and with the use of his powerful arms he could push his bowl along the streets. His haunts were around Manor Street and the lanes of Oxmantown. Billy Davis became too fond of drink and then started to rob people. He spent several short terms of imprisonment in Newgate Jail. One

THE OLD WAYS

of the Dublin street ballads, 'The Twangman's Revenge', sung by 'Zozimus', had the lines

> He took her out to Sandymount
> To hear the waters rowl
> And he won the heart of the Twangman's mot
> Playing Billy in the Bowl.

Poor Billy! While robbing a man, he also killed him. A witness saw Billy sliding away in his bowl. Billy was arrested, sentenced to life imprisonment and he died in jail.

♥ ♥ ♥

'All Parcels' was a beggar lady who spent every day collecting waste paper. She would make it up into several neat parcels and was a familiar sight carrying her bundles round the Liberties. Her usual haunts were Thomas Street and James's Street. Waste paper in those days, the 1930s, was valuable, and a good sack-full of six parcels would be worth a few pennies each day. As children, we collected waste paper for picture money, for the Fourpenny Rush. 'All Parcels' collected it to keep herself alive.

♥ ♥ ♥

Lilian McEvoy was a Dublin street musician who used to play in O'Connell Street about 1928. The police moved her along, so she then played in Earl Street. The police moved her again and she took up another stand in Marlborough Street, outside Gogan's shop at the corner of North Earl Street. Gogan's shop was used by Michael Collins and other IRA leaders during the Black and Tan War as a depot for despatches.

Lilian later moved to Grafton Street and one evening in 1932 she was spotted and heard by Fritz Kreisler, the world-famous violinist. He was in Dublin for an engagement in the Theatre Royal. Kreisler, who had spent his life helping good street musicians, got Lilian a week's engagement in the The-

*One of Dublin's characters –
Davy Stephens, who sold newspapers in Dun Laoghaire.*

atre Royal. That week, which took Lilian off the cold winter streets of Dublin, was the start of a famous stage career and she never had to play in the streets again.

Lilian then went to England and married a man named Douglas. Her daughter, Shirley Douglas, followed her mother's stage tradition and Shirley's record, 'Freight Train', is well-known to skiffle group fans. The next time you hear Shirley's records, think of her mother, the young girl from Kells, County Meath, who went to fame and fortune from Grafton Street, Dublin.

Dublin had many other characters. Here are a few of their names – Dunlavin, Hamlet, Jack the Tumbler, Uncle, Rock, Damn the Weather, Prince of Denmark, Hairy Lemon, Hairy Yank, Shell-Shock Joe, The Toucher Doyle,

THE OLD WAYS

Bugler Dunne, Jembo-no-Toes, the Blind Artillery Man, Johnny Forty Coats, Mad Mary, the Professor and Davy Stephens.

Dublin still has many characters and I'm sure that every Dubliner has his own favourites. You know who I mean – 'yer man' in the bookies office, at the football match, on the bus or marking his card at a game of bingo. Whenever you turn a corner in Dublin, you're sure to meet a host of characters. Of course, we have some lovely jewel-and-darlin' lady characters as well, like 'yer wan' in Moore Street. They have wit at their finger-tips. Talk to them and get the real feel of Dublin. Too many tourists and natives miss all this life as they move through the streets of Dublin.

SOME DUBLIN SLANG

IF 'ZOZIMUS' WAS ALIVE TODAY he'd have to employ an interpreter. No one would understand him and his 'Newgate Cant'. If he said: 'He was sweating his duds to ris it,' his interpreter would have to explain that 'Zozimus' was going to pawn his clothes to raise a few shillings. The old Newgate slang had a beauty all its own and can be found in the ballads 'Luke Caffrey's Ghost', 'De Night before Larry was Stretched', 'Mrs Coffey', 'Larry's Ghost' and 'The Kilmainham Minuet'.

The Joly collection of song music in the National Library is well worth a case study. The Luke Caffrey in the ballad was arrested in Ram Alley beside Skinner's Row, opposite Christ Church Cathedral. The crowd said: 'If Luke hadn't of let the watch take him, they'd have skinned him alive.' Luke put up a great fight. 'He squar'd up to de two baillies, tipp'd wan of dem a lovin' squeeze, den gave him a cut of bread an' butter over de elbow. De fight went on an' den he tipp'd de odder a long-arm leg, mid a dig in the smellers dat laid him on his face, be de hokey! After Luke was hanged, his ghost cem back lookin' like nuttin' on earth. His eyes were swelled in his brain-box, like two scalded goose-berries in a mutton tart and his grinders rattled in his jaw-wags for all de world like a pair of white-headed fortune-tellers in an elbow-shaker's bone box.' Luke wanted to tell his friends to lay off his girl-friend, who was known as 'One-eyed Bid of de alley' and he threatened the boys that if they were at Bid he'd 'whitewash the walls with their brains'. Luke was hanged in Kilmainham with his face towards the city.

Larry was hanged (stretched) in Newgate Jail. His wife Nell was comforted by Katto Crawley who 'tipped de bottle down Nell's t'rottle, which opened de lights in her garret. Nell cursed de bloody old judge who gev de cramp-jaw to her Larry.' She also cursed Gregg the jailer in Newgate Jail who broke up her last visit with Larry and put all the prisoners in their cage. Years later, Gregg kicked a street-girl to death because she accused him of murdering Oliver Bond in 1798. 'I see'd ye,' she said. 'I see'd ya. Ya hit him on the scruff of de head wid a copper kittle.'

'Zozimus' was the King of the Newgate Cant, 'Have yis no other de varnishin' only stickin' pins in a dark man. If de watch was set or de nu po-liss out, I'd make some iv ye jump. Jim Crow, I feel horrible wet. Am I standin' in a poddel, Stoney?'

Down the years, the Newgate Cant, Dublin slang and expressions changed with education. Yet quite a few of the old traditional ones remain. The boss is known as *the head buck cat; fla-hool-ack*, from the Irish 'flathuil', means 'generous'; *Box the Fox,* to rob an orchard; the *Jer* and *mitch*, staying away from school; *stag* is an informer (Major Sirr's stag house, Kilmainham); *biffed,* slapped with a leather strap; *stocious*, drunk; *jewel-an'-darlin'* is a phrase used by Dublin women mostly to other women; *mal-a-Voke* or '*I'll mal-a-voke ya'* is a Dublin war cry, usually a woman's; *Red Biddy* was a lethal mixture of methylated spirits and Brasso; *wizent* refers to a small child with an older child's face, as in '*He's a wizent ol' man, missus*'; a *hussy* is a loose girl or a girl that wore lipstick years ago. Another insulting phrase was: '*A bitch is a dog, a decent dog, but you, ye pup, ye're nuttin'.*

THE OLD WAYS

Here are some examples of the way some Dubliners pronounce words: pennert for a pennyworth; *joca-la* for chocolate; *ospidal* for hospital; *ceilent* for ceiling; *Eammont* for the name Eamonn; *trun it* for threw it; *bruid* for bread. *None more bein' gev out* means that there's nothing more being handed out; *Stee-ven-ziz* refers to Dr Steeven's Hospital; *orators* means auditors.

The modern *ben lang* or slang is also changing and the experts may find that some of it has got mixed up with Cockney rhyming slang. You will still hear the following: *corn-beef* for chief; *bit-an-brace* for face; *mince pies* for eyes; *two-by-four* for a door; *plates of meat* for feet; *fork and knife* for wife; *apples and pears* for stairs; *whistle and flute* for a suit of clothes. The older words were *clobber* or *duds* and the English slang for suit is *tin of fruit*. The priest is known as the *sky pilot*. *On the ball* is begging. A *lid* is a hat; *German band* a hand; *strides* are trousers and *jam-jar* a car.

One and One, which means fish and chips, dates from the days the 'Eyeties' (Italians) couldn't speak English so the Dubliners pointed: 'Wan of that and wan of that'.

The Italians caught on quickly and from a small beginning as instrument-makers in the 18th century, they are all over Dublin now and at one time they owned much of O'Connell Street. There was also an area in the Liberties known as 'Little Italy'.

The Bay-No was a children's play centre set up by the Iveagh Trust. It is now a vocational shool. *Husband and wife* or *out in a box* means life imprisonment; a *peter* is a safe; *morning dew* or *screw* a prison officer; *four by two* a Jew; *one by two* a shoe. A *Kevin Barry* stands for a brave person; *a long-distance man* is one who stops in the best hotels for one night and leaves next morning with the best silver. *Working the oracle, pulling rabbits out of a hat* or *pulling a quick one* all mean roughly the same thing.

A wagon, a nut, a head case, a lu-la, a fruit-'n'-nut, stir crazy all refer to a mad man, but each phrase has a subtlety all its own. *A paraffin lamp* means

ME JEWEL AND DARLIN' DUBLIN

a tramp; *a chicken's neck* is a dud; *to croak* is to die; *the Naller* is the canal; *the flicks* are the pictures (cinema). A *claud* or *a wing* means a penny and *a make* is a halfpenny. *He's not the full shilling*, *He's touched* or *He's not all there* means he's crazy. *Mouth organs* are pigs' feet; *stubbed* means no response at the door and a *rat* is a mean person.

Under the hammer was a term used in coal-yards when workers did not earn the full minimum wage. *Drum and gaff* refers to housebreaking. *Richard the Third* or *a bird* is a girl. *Collecting a flake* means picking up cigarette butts from the gutter. *A pavement hostess* is a street-girl and *guino* is money. *The Holy Hour* refers to the hour (2.30 to 3.30 p.m.) when public-houses close their doors to get the people home for their dinners. This closing hour was passed by law. *Skedaddle* is an order to move along.

Back again to the rhyming slang. Here are more examples. *A battle cruiser* is a *boozer* or public-house. *Peggy Dell* is a cell; *Teddy bear* is hair; *Uncle Ned* is head; *Donald Pears* is ears; *bars in the grate* are teeth; *North and South* the mouth; *rambling rose* the nose; *scotch-peg* the leg; *needle and thread* is bed; *bottle and stoppers* are the police (coppers). *Joe Skinner* means dinner; *Belinda Lee* tea; *King Farouks* are books; *linen drapers* are papers. A *bull and cow* is a row; *daisy roots* are boots; *Tom Dick* means sick; *Nelson Eddies*, *readies* and *bees and honey* all stand for money. *Town Hall* refers to football; *skin and blister* is a sister; *one and other* a brother. *Cain and Abel* is a table; *tit for tat* is a chat; *laughing jokes* are smokes; *ship's hatches* are matches; *kitchen range* is change; *sky rocket* is pocket; *roast joint* a pint; *mother and daughter* is water.

A mixture of Irish and English and old-time slang is used widely today and a *gansey load* in the 1930s still means a gansey load to the childer of 1974 – your jersey full of apples after a night at the ol' *Box the Fox*.

'Do you know what I'm going to tell ya, Mister T.? Like, ya know like, I'm gone off me food. I'm not the same man at all, at all. No, it's me liver, like, giving me hell. As the Missus says: Doctors differ and patients die. Well, Mr T., they can differ all they *bloodywelllike* but none of them is doing the

THE OLD WAYS

damn thing any good, me liver, I mean.' The man with the bad liver spreads six cream buns on the wooden seat of the workers' hut, then he opens a tin of sardines and sticks a few into each cream bun and sprinkles each bun with a drop of fish oil, fills his jam-jar with tea and eats and drinks the lot in four minutes flat. Then he says: 'Naw, didn't enjoy it. I'm really gone off me food. The liver is a terrible thing. It's worser nor the heart. Why does it have to be me, Mister T.? Like, ya know like, I'm no bowsie, gurrier or gowger. I take care of me health, like. I'm very fussy about what I eat and drink.' Another Dubliner comes on the scene and says to the man with the bad liver: 'I don't want to worry ya, like, Pat. Far be it from me to worry ya, but that bloody liver's goin' to kill ya, like, and I know be the *lookofya* that yer gone off yer food. Ah well, as long as ya keep the roof over yer head, that's all that matters. Amn't I right, Mister T.? Keep the roof over yer head and *yalbe* as happy as Larry.'

I often wondered who was Larry and why was he always happy. Was it Larry the Lockman at the second lock on the Grand Canal, Goldenbridge? Or was it Larry Burn of Glenmalure House, Rialto, who had the only public-house in Dublin where the grass grew under your feet as you stood at the bar. However, just before the lawn had fully grown between the floor-boards, Larry sold out and a modern pub marks the historic site today. 'Happy as Larry'. Well, we can be sure it wasn't Larry the night before he was stretched.

But then everyone wasn't always happy. 'See yer man. He has a face that would stop a clock' or 'Yer man, he has a face like a plateful of mortal sins.' I don't think anyone in the world can tell what a mortaller (mortal sin) looks like. But the Dubliner – ah well, they're different, like. They can tell ya what a 'plateful of mortal sins' looks like!

SOUNDS, SMELLS AND COLOURS

LISTEN TO DUBLIN. LISTEN TO ITS HEART BEATING, its children laughing or crying. Listen for the Dalymount roar or the cultured cry from the GAA

ME JEWEL AND DARLIN' DUBLIN

crowds in Croke Park. Listen to the dealers in the streets and the jingle sounds of silver and copper coins in their apron pockets. Listen for the footsteps of the odd horse-car going over grey cobblestones, or seagulls screeching over waste-bins at Mountjoy prison or around the fishing boats at Howth Harbour.

The sounds of church-bells ringing, clocks striking, rivers and canals flowing and the sound of a train, the foghorn and the factory hooter. Listen for the sound of Dublin wit wherever Dubliners are gathered. The fire brigade and ambulance services lead the way in Dublin siren sounds. The steel demolition ball crushing to dust our historic houses and electric hammers dancing on our streets and roads are not far behind. Listen, too, to the sound of silence in the Hollow in the Phoenix Park after the band and the people have gone home and to the strange foreign sounds from the cages and pits in Dublin Zoo.

The sounds of Dublin are changing daily. Gone forever are the old familiar magical sounds of *Coal blocks, coal blocks, what do you feed your mother on?*

Looking towards Jameson's Distillery on Bow Street.

THE OLD WAYS

Herrilly Mail, Herrilly Mail. (This call stood for '*Herald* and *Mail*', the two Dublin evening papers. Though the '*Mail*' has folded long ago, the '*Herald*' is still very much alive.) *Stop Press, Stop Press. Read all about it. Sweet Lavender, Water Cress. Taffey Apples, Taffey Apples, get your windy mills, rags, bottles, jam-jars and bones, windy mills and bones.*

The ringing of the coal-man's bell tied to the horse's head has been replaced by central heating which brings us to the smells of Dublin, when the boiler breaks down or goes haywire.

'Go down to Moore Street', said the late Jimmy O'Dea, the Dublin comedian, 'and get your nose educated.' Nose education in Dublin is second to none in the world. To qualify for a diploma you had to be able to stand on Ward Hill in the Liberties and see if your nose could cope with the smell from O'Keefe's the knackers' yard, and be able to tell the difference between the smells from the Liffey's forty shades of green, each with its own peculiar smell.

Ah, but there were other smells in Dublin, smells as sweet as honey or as fragrant as new-mown hay, like the smell of Jacob's biscuits in Bishop Street, Willwood jams in Parnell Street or Mackintosh's chocolate in Kilmainham. Alas, these have all gone now, as have the smell of pig-yards in the gardens of Georgian mansions or Cooper's horse stables in Queen Street, which would have reminded you of the Horse Show in Ballsbridge. Until recently, you could still smell the hops and porter at James's Gate or, if you preferred the hard tack, you went over to Hangman's Lane and walked slowly towards Smithfield and the Red Cow. You could nearly smell yourself drunk! And don't forget the smell of the fish-and-chipper on a cold winter's night; sometimes they even smelt better than they tasted!

You could inhale for your life's worth the odour of the fish and fruit markets or children at the pictures eating crisps, popcorn and oranges. You could wallow in the smell of Lemon's sweets on the banks of the Tolka and it didn't have to be a Saturday either. Strawberry, raspberry, pineapple, greengage, you

ME JEWEL AND DARLIN' DUBLIN

Above: The Fruit and Vegetable Market off Capel Street. The drawing shows the main entrance crowned with the arms of Dublin. It was erected in 1892. Nearby is the Fish Market and also the Daisy Market. Below: Can you imagine the smell and the noise of cattle being driven down Red Cow Lane towards Smithfield? The chimney at the end is part of Jameson's distillery.

name the flavour and there you could smell it.

Of course, you can still enjoy the aroma from Bewley's shops when the coffee is being ground or brewed or just displayed in the windows like small brown mountains. At Hallowe'en you can smell Bewley's barm-bracks all over Dublin. The man on the bus with a sup too much, the new-born babe in its mother's arms, incense and candles burning while people pray together at the countless shrines – they all make up the smells of Dublin, the nice ones and the bitter ones.

The pork butchers with their meats, sausages, peppers and seasonings, the fresh bread from the bakery, a rasher-and egg frying on a shovel over a coke fire in a watchman's hut are enough to make your tongue water. What are your favourite smells of Dublin? Or do you leave all that sort of thing to the Bisto Kids?

What colour is Dublin city? Gold, silver and battleship grey, or rich warm red and brown, blue skies speckled with large and small green domes and grey spires. Transparent windows in a million office blocks with bronze and brass-coloured name plates and letter boxes. Or the multi-coloured wall of a Capel Street shop and the black-and-white pillars of the old Parliament House, lovingly cleaned in the past few years. The ever-changing colours of Dame Street. Trinity College is like a framed picture with its white window-frames surrounded by the rich greys of expert stonework. The green-leaved trees along the banks of the Liffey are reflected in the changing colours

This strange archway leads to Cooper's of Queen Street, which was once a horse dealers.

of her waters. Observe the golden letters and harp on the Parnell Monument and the statue of Mr Gray watching the colourful scene at Abbey Street corner.

The mountains of black diamonds in Dublin Port used to provide heat for half the city. The red-and-grey gasometers, contrasting with the blue-and-yellow buoys near the Baily Lighthouse and the grey-and-white majestic Custom House, which is Dublin's glory on a sunny day, are, alas, no more.

Now, at night, the neon lights provide movement and colour. The first illuminated sign I remember seeing in Dublin was the Bovril sign high over College Green. What a spectacle it was as it burst into a rainbow of colours.

The silver-studded wood on the Ha'penny Bridge, which dated from 1816, is now covered by tarmacadam sheets, which is a pity. There was something old and solid about the wood and its shiny studs, but it did get very slippery in wet weather. Not far from the bridge is the spot where Hector Grey stood on a Sunday morning, selling his wares. Hector is now dead, but his stand is still used and his shop in Liffey Street is now run by his sons.

Undoubtedly the most interesting aspect of Dublin is its people. Men, women and children, they are colourful in speech and manner and only waiting to give a smile and have a chat with a friend or a visitor.

DUBLIN'S OLD NEWSPAPERS

IF YOU EVER GET BORED, fed up or, as a Dubliner would say, 'browned-off', you could go down to the National Library in Kildare Street, climb the stone staircase, push in the door and ask 'yer man' behind the counter to let you have a look at *The Dublin Penny Journal*, *The Freeman's Journal*, the old *Irish Times Weekly*, *Dublin Evening Post* or *The Dublin Chronicle*. Today, you need a library ticket to enter, but anyone can apply for a visitor's ticket. Ask for *The Correspondent*, a paper which firmly supported the establishment. It was printed in the early 1800s, firstly by E. Dowling of 1a College Green, and later by J. Martin at 11 Fleet Street. *The Comet*, a Sunday paper, first

THE OLD WAYS

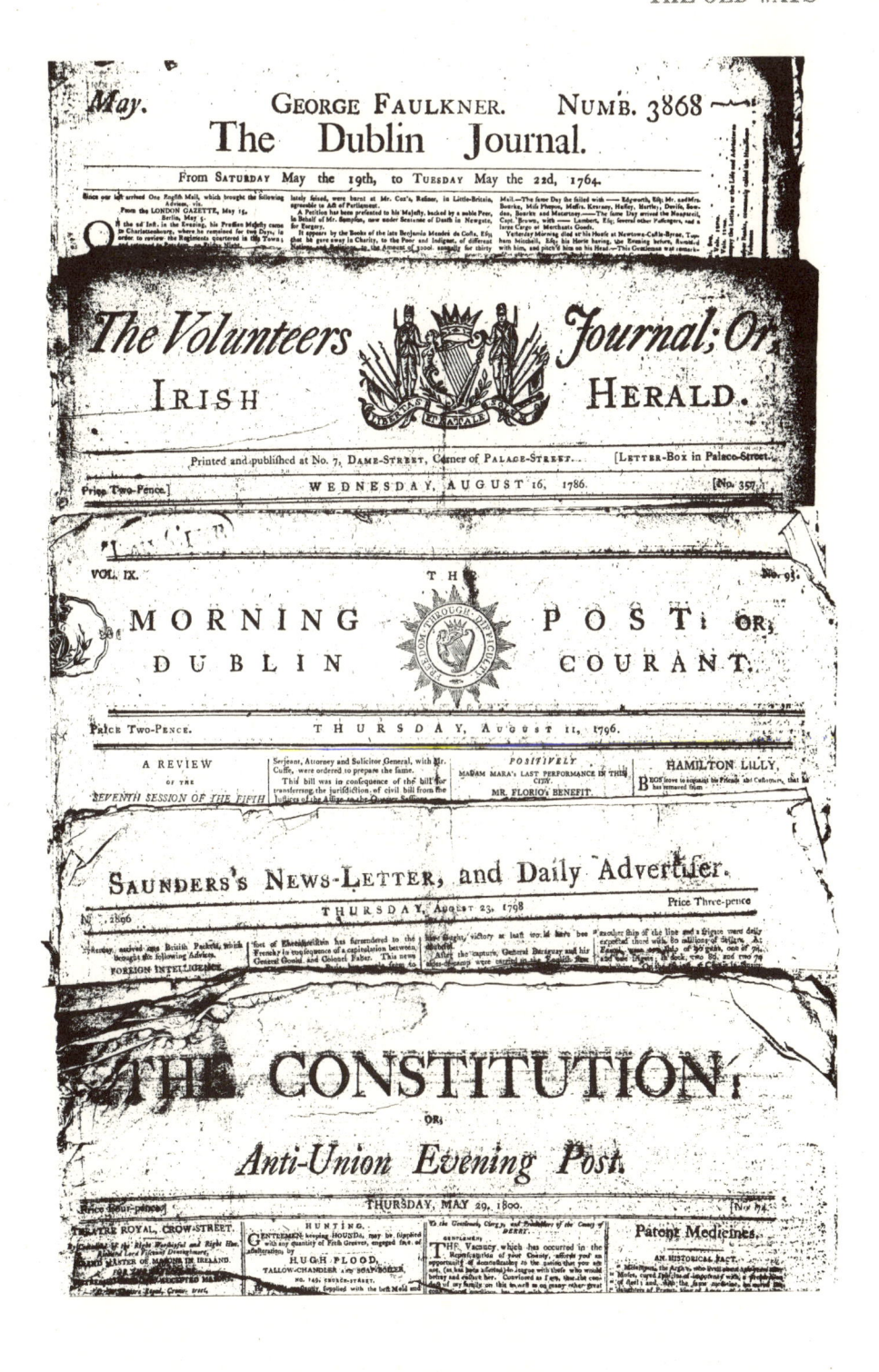

The Dublin Journal
GEORGE FAULKNER. NUMB. 3868
May.
From Saturday May the 19th, to Tuesday May the 22d, 1764.

The Volunteers Journal; Or, Irish Herald.
Printed and published at No. 7, DAME-STREET, Corner of PALACE-STREET. [LETTER-BOX in Palace-Street.
[Price Two-Pence.] WEDNESDAY, AUGUST 16, 1786. [No. 357.

THE MORNING POST; OR, DUBLIN COURANT.
PRICE TWO-PENCE. THURSDAY, AUGUST 11, 1796.

Saunders's News-Letter, and Daily Advertiser.
THURSDAY, August 23, 1798. Price Three-pence.

THE CONSTITUTION;
OR,
Anti-Union Evening Post
THURSDAY, MAY 29, 1800.

ME JEWEL AND DARLIN' DUBLIN

The Patriot
WEDNESDAY, DECEMBER 7, 1814.

The Star,
AND FASHIONABLE WORLD.
DUBLIN, MONDAY, OCTOBER 11, 1824.

The Irish Independent
TRADE AND LABOUR JOURNAL.
VOL. I.—No. 5.   DUBLIN, SATURDAY, OCTOBER 11, 1873.

The Irishman.
VOL. XVIII.—NO 12   DUBLIN SATURDAY, SEPTEMBER 25, 1875.

THE IRISH VOLUNTEER
an t-Óglác
Vol. 1. No. 19.   Saturday, June 13, 1914   Price, 1d.

appeared on 1 May 1831, one of its aims being to keep an uncompromising eye 'upon ecclesiastical hypocrisy, cant and humbug'. It was printed by Brown & Sheehan at 10 D'Olier Street. Ask also for young Paddy Kelly's *Budget*. The magic of the papers will soon have you in wonderland. I'll bet the next time you go, you will bring a great big notebook and a few biros. Now if you are feeling depressed and want to get your spirit and your blood up, well then ask for *The Nation*, *The Irish Felon* or the *Eye Opener*. The editor of *Eye Opener* was a man named McIntyre. He was by no means a Republican and his paper contained a good few anti-Irish articles. Nevertheless, he was arrested in 1916 and taken prisoner to Portobello Barracks, where he was murdered along with Sheehy-Skeffington and another man named Kelly. None of the three men was in any way connected with the 1916 Rising.

Also ask for *Zozimus* and *The Irish People*, the Fenian newspaper, or John Mitchel's *United Irishman* (1848), the *Wolfe Tone Weekly* or *An Phoblacht*. Someone said one time that Dubliners speak and spend words like sailors. Well, you can take my word for it, they wrote them for the sailors of the world. And newspapers were not ten a penny either; in fact, they were a bit on the expensive side. *The Nation* newspaper was sixpence in 1842; other papers were fourpence each or eight camacks or four clauds or four wings or eight makes, all of which added up to four old pence.

The written word was always in demand in Dublin. The first newspapers appeared in the 16th century and were a small type of almanac, which told you the type of dinner you were going to have in three weeks' time. Star-gazing was a popular art and all the future visions were recorded in words. In the early 17th century, *Pue's Occurrences* appeared and was accepted as the official organ of Dublin. Next on the scene was *Dublin Intelligence*. The first Republican revolutionary newspaper to reach the streets of Dublin was the Belfast-printed and published *Northern Star*, official organ of the United Irishmen. This was edited by Samuel Neilson and distributed by Dr Brennan in Dame Street, under the eyes of Dublin Castle.

The Nation newspaper, founded by the Young Irelanders – Davis, Duffy and Dillon – moved a little further away to Abbey Street where *The Independent* Newspapers' offices stand today. John Mitchell wasn't too fussy about the Castle. His office was in Trinity Street but his paper, *The United Irishman*, lasted only for six issues before it was suppressed and he himself sent in chains to Van Diemen's Land. *The Irish Felon*, edited by Thomas Delvin Reilly and John Martin, was also printed in Trinity Street and it, too, was suppressed and its editors jailed.

'Damn the Castle', said Thomas Clarke Luby, editor of *The Irish People*, organ of the Fenian Brotherhood, as he sat at his desk in their offices at 12 Parliament Street. O'Donovan Rossa was the business manager, but it wasn't long until the Castle troops raided and suppressed the paper and sent Clarke, Luby and Rossa to penal servitude for twenty years in British dungeons. *Zozimus* (1870), started by A.M. Sullivan from the *Nation* office in Abbey Street, got its name and cover from Michael Moran, the blind ballad singer, whom we have already met. The cover showed 'Zozimus' chasing English comics out of Ireland. Pimlico, Charlemont Street and Liberty Hall were the places where Connolly edited and wrote his *Workers' Republic*, the organ of the Irish Citizen Army. *The Irish Volunteer*, which gave details of history and the trade of arms for war, was published at 65 Middle Abbey Street, Dublin. In the 1913-1914 issues there are some very interesting articles on the Irish Volunteers of 1782 and an article by The O'Rahilly on the flag colours for every county in Ireland. This article was written as a suggestion to each Volunteer Company to enable them to design their own Brigade flags.

From the Dublin Central Wolfe Tone Club Committee (IRB) came the idea for *The Irish Freedom* newspaper. Tom Clarke and Sean MacDiarmada, both executed in 1916, were the guiding lights. Tom acted as chairman and Sean as treasurer on the editorial committee. The first issue was on sale on 1

November 1910. The editorial address was given at 7 Sinnot Place, off Dorset Street. Later the offices were moved to 5 Findlater's Place and in May 1914 the office was again moved, this time to 12 D'Olier Street. Among the contributors were Patrick Pearse and Terence McSwiney. McSwiney died on hunger strike in Brixton Prison in October 1920 after a 75-day fast. Pat McCartan was editor. Most of the work and contacts made were at Tom Clarke's shop at 75A Parnell Street. An old photograph shows the small shop with Tom at the door.

T. S. O'Cléirig / Tom Clarke, Tobacconist & Stationer

The shop window had the number 75A in the centre and also stated 'Branch at 55 Amiens Street'. Newspaper posters outside the shop read as follows:

Irish Freedom
The Principles of Freedom

The Principles of Freedom was Terence McSwiney's book, then available in pamphlet form. Next came an advertisement for *Tit-Bits, Ireland's Own, Boxing World, Daily Sketch* and, on the far side, posters for *The Diamond, Racing Judge* and *The Irish Times*, which gives some idea of the reading matter that was available at the period.

A hundred years ago there were more comics and papers written and printed in Dublin than in London. The old *Thoms' Directory* of 1917 lists 127 Dublin printed and published papers and pamphlets covering every aspect of life and religion. Even a brief study of old copies of *The Irish Builder, Shamrock and Emerald, Irish Citizen* and the *Catholic Bulletin* (published by Gills), which was the first to record in detail the full account of the 1916 Easter Week Rising, would be rewarding. The other masterpiece on 1916 is the *Irish Times' Sinn Féin Rebellion Handbook,* which contains a full report of the British Commission set up after the Rising. Many of the books on the 1916 Rising were written from these two sources.

The Irish Times is Dublin's and Ireland's oldest daily newspaper and its slogan is 'If you miss *The Irish Times* you miss part of the day'. It is also good to see that we still have *Ireland's Own* with us. Published in Wexford, it is loaded with information and light reading, which includes the Pen Pals' Corner. Its slogan is 'The week wouldn't be the same without *Ireland's Own*'. *Our Boys* was another paper dating back to the pre-1916 period and was mainly sold in schools.

Another source of great amusement and information is the advertisements. It is nice to come across an old advertisement for a business still in existence. And how strange and quaint they sound today. It is also a surprise to see announcements of hundreds and hundreds of firms now closed down and to note the strange trades, products and activities long since forgotten.

Faulkner's Journal was a dullish newspaper which could always be relied upon to support the establishment. It had a long history stretching back to the middle of the 18th century and continued till 1825 when it was bought up by *The Irish Times*. Faulkner's had an extensive publishing business and they printed and published many interesting books. Their offices and works were at 27 Parliament Street. This street provided a home for many newspapers and printers over the years. In addition to *the Irish People* already mentioned, *The Daily Express* in 1917 had offices at 39 and 40 and, at the corner, a few doors up were the offices and works of the daily *Evening Mail*. 'Herrilly Mail … Paper, sir. Paper, sir. Herrilly Mail.' Dublin lost something when the old *Evening Mail* closed down. At one time they brought out a weekly paper as well. The *Evening Mail* was always regarded as a Protestant paper, yet if you were looking for a job, it was always the long columns of 'Situations Vacant' in the *Mail* everyone turned to. If you felt sore about anything, it was to the *Evening Mail* you sent your letter. 'Write to the *Mail* about it' became as familiar as senna pods or the Bovril sign in College Green. I even remember one time winning £5 on the *Evening Mail* leading article (editorial). Coupons were a

THE OLD WAYS

shilling each, the same as football or horse-racing.

The first thing we looked at in the *Mail* was the title of the leading article. Then we read Mandrake the Magician (cartoon) and over to the letters page. Whether you agreed or not, the *Mail* always spoke out in the honest Huguenot tradition of its famous owner-editor, Joseph Sheridan Le Fanu, who took over the paper in 1842. He was born at 45 Dominick Street on 28 August, 1814. He studied law at Trinity College but, as soon as he graduated, he changed the wig and gown for the quill and ink. He wrote several books and can be truly acclaimed as Dublin's Edgar Allan Poe for his brilliant ghost stories.

He also bought the *Dublin University Magazine* and it was in this magazine that his serial story, *The House by the Churchyard*, first appeared under the pen name Charles de Cresseron. The setting was the house and churchyard in Chapelizod where he spent his childhood days. He died in 70 Merrion Square in 1873.

Gone forever is the old 'Stop Press, Stop Press. Read all about it. Stop Press. Herrilly Mail, Herrilly Mail. Paper, sir. Paper,' 'Sorry, I can't read.' 'Well, ya can look at the bloody pictures, can't ya?'

Many papers and comics went out of existence because they took a strong political stand. The one that had no worries in this direction was *The Dublin Gazette*, which was printed and published every Tuesday and Thursday from 8 and 9 Crow Street by the King's authority! This paper was started by King James II in 1689 but after he disappeared from the scene the paper ceased to appear. Sixteen years later another *Dublin Gazette* ('Published by authority') appeared at The Custom House Printing Office at Crane Lane, off Dame Street.

Fish and chips wrapped in a sheet of newspaper provides eating, reading and education and you need no fancy firelighters when you have a paper handy. I've seen them used for many purposes – tablecloths, blankets on tramps in the Phoenix Park, across the chest or under the coat to keep out the wind and rain, or for making small cone-shaped bags for sweets or monkey nuts. I've made them into dolls for little girls and aeroplanes or Napoleon hats for little boys.

Dublin has a great tradition in the written word. It's a far cry from quill and ink to the modern printing and colour presses of today. The Dublin writers of old claimed they were the true successors of the Bards of Di, Goddess of the Moon, and many used the pen name 'Lady Di'. My favourite Lady Di today is Nell McCafferty, the Derry journalist.

CHAPTER 3

OLD DUBLIN TOWN

DUBLIN'S MANY LIBERTIES

Thomas Court and Donore

THOMAS STREET, DUBLIN, gets its name from Thomas-à-Becket, the martyred Archbishop of Canterbury. It was the murder of Becket which gave Dublin its first Liberty. King Henry II came to Ireland in the year 1171. His army marched to Dublin where he spent the Christmas season. One day he rode out to St Catherine's Church and picked a site of land beside it. 'Here,' he said, 'let an abbey be founded and dedicated to our holy martyr.' He then gave the lease of lands to the Victorine Canons to build their abbey. He also gave them a special Liberty owing allegiance to no one but God and the King.

Six years later Laurence O'Toole laid the foundation-stone and the first Abbot was William Fitz-Adlem. The Abbey soon spread out to take in the lands of Donore and so became known as the Liberty of Thomas Court and Donore. This royal foundation received royal grants and other charters, giving it more lands and property throughout the country and making it the wealthiest and most powerful in Ireland. It had its own palace, church, courts, gallows, prisons, graveyard and orchard gardens. Later it diverted the city water supply and had its own watercourse and mills. It gathered taxes and also had

Children at play in the Liberties – Grey Street looking towards Meath Street.

fishing rights on the River Liffey. Strongbow's sister, Basila, ended her days in its guesthouse. King John later confirmed Henry's Liberty and issued a charter to this effect.

Myles de Cogan and Hugh de Lacy both gave large grants of land and gold to the Abbey and, in his will, de Lacy bequeathed all his wealth and property to it, asking that his body be buried in its vaults. However, after he was killed in action at Durrow, the monks of Bective Abbey, County Meath, took his body and buried it in their own churchyard. The Abbot of Thomas Court and Donore was furious and demanded that the body be brought to Dublin. The monks in Bective refused and a great row developed. In an attempt at compromise, the Bective monks cut off de Lacy's head and sent it to Dublin. This only made matters worse. The Abbot of St Thomas's went to the courts, a commission was set up and after several years the rest of the body was sent to Dublin. The Bective churchyard can still be seen today, while there is no trace whatsoever of de Lacy in the graves or vaults of St Thomas's Abbey.

Earl of Meath's Liberty

On 31 March, 1539, the Abbey, its lands, property, malt mills and double mills were handed over lock, stock and barrel for ever to William Brabazon, the King's Chancellor and Treasurer in Ireland, at an annual rent of 18s. 6d. The Abbey church was suppressed on 30 October, 1540. The Brabazons later became the Barons of Ardee and later still Earls of Meath. This is how the area got its name, The Earl of Meath's Liberty.

The Liberty lands in Dublin took in Dolphin's Barn, Harold's Cross, James's Street, Pimlico, Marrowbone Lane, Meath Street, Bridgefoot Street, Thomas Street and all the lanes and alleys in the neighbourhood. Within these confines are numerous dwellings steeped in history. The infamous Debtors' Prison was beside Emmet's depot in Marshalsea Lane and nearby was 151-153 Thomas Street, where Lord Edward Fitzgerald was arrested. The owner of this house, Nicholas Murphy, was also arrested and became penniless as a result of his loyalty to Lord Edward.

At St Catherine's in Thomas Street, Robert Emmet was hanged and beheaded on 20 September, 1803. The funerals of the Young Irelanders and the Fenian chiefs and brave Tom Ashe stopped here for a moment on their way to Glasnevin Cemetery. James Connolly once lived in Pimlico, an area that was formerly part of the Abbey grounds.

The White Bull Inn was one of the many old drinking houses with interesting names, long since vanished. Here in Thomas Street the rebels of 1798 and 1803 met, a few doors from Nicholas Murphy's house. The Black Bull Inn was just at the corner of Bridgefoot Street nearby. It was here in 1766 that two pirates were captured and later hanged on Misery Hill. Their names were McKinlie and Gidley. Together with a man named Zekerman and another named St Quintin, they took over the *Sandwick* at sea and made off with her cargo of gold ingots and dust, jewels and Spanish milled dollars. They were traced from Wexford where they landed and were arrested, first in New Ross and later at the Black Bull Inn.

The Yellow Bottle Inn, near where Thomas Street Library stood, was another favourite meeting-place of the United Irishmen. Then there was the Pipers' Club, also in Thomas Street, where you could hear beautiful Irish music on a Saturday night, or on any night for that matter. For this was Potts, Rowesome and Seery country, where fine musicians gathered and played their Irish traditional airs in the ancient lands of Dublin's first liberty.

Ailred's Liberty

The second Liberty of Dublin came from Rome. In the year 1188, Ailred the Dane and his wife returned to their home which was just outside the Newgate Wall in Dublin. They had been on a pilgrimage to the Holy Land and when they entered Dublin by St Audoen's Arch they both carried sprays of palm.

An ancient site in Thomas Street – the unusual entrance to Kelly's Timber Yard, now owned by Chadwick's Ltd.

From that day on, he was known as Ailred the Palmer. He also owned lands in Rathmines and Chapelizod and this is how we get the names of Palmerstown and Palmerston.

Ailred and his wife were many years married but were childless. Three days after they returned home, Ailred told his wife that he was going to become a priest. 'Oh you are, are ye,' the wife said or words to that effect. 'Well, bedad, if ye do I'll become a nun.' 'It's agreed,' he said. 'What order or rule will we adopt?' 'The rule of St Augustine,' she said. 'We will open a hospital,' said Ailred, 'a hospital of St John, like the one in the Holy City.'

In the year 1151, John Hircan, Prince of the Jews, ordered that a leper hospital be built at the Tower of Tancred near St Eithne's Gate in Jerusalem. This was the first hospital of its kind in the world. Ailred and his wife founded the second in Thomas Street, where John's Lane Church stands today. Ailred the prior and his monks nursed and cared for the sick, while the nuns made the vestments for the Canons of Dublin and also cooked the food and cleaned the hospital.

Ailred received his Liberty from Pope Clement III. This put the hospital and priory completely under Rome and exempt from the city's jurisdiction. Ailred's Liberty took in his own lands of Thomas Street and part of Francis Street and Vicar Street. On the other side, the lands were bordered by the Liffey and the city walls. The hospital continued to thrive until the year 1540. Kelly's timber yard, which is now Chadwick's Ltd., opposite John's Lane Church, was the priory graveyard, where the remains of Ailred, his wife and many other holy followers of St Augustine lie today.

The Augustinians were on the run for 240 years and have a magnificent history which would fill many books. Their present church, called by John Ruskin 'a poem in stone', was built by Fenian stonemasons and labourers. The clerk of works on the job was none other than the Pagan O'Leary, the great Fenian, who said: 'We were better men when we were pagans. 'Tis a pity St

Patrick ever found us.' The impressive entrance is in Thomas Street.

A few doors away from Chadwick's stood the public-house where James Connolly founded his Socialist Party. Still to be seen today is Vicar Street Guardhouse, where the bodies of Lord Kilwarden and his nephew were brought after their carriage was attacked in the Emmet Rising. Vicar Street also held the city labour yard, where poor men and women had to do a hard day's work for a bowl of soup and a hunk of bread.

In John's Lane, beside the church, Anne Devlin lived in a garret before moving to Little Elbow Lane in the Coombe. Behind the church stands Mullinahack, a corruption of *muilleann salach* (dirty mill) from the waters coming down Dirty Lane (Bridgefoot Street). This is another place in Dublin where you can feel and sense the past.

On a plot of ground (Francis Street) owned by Ralph le Porter, an order of Franciscans or Grey Friars was founded in the year 1235. This church later became the church of St Nicholas of Myra, the poorest religious house in Dublin, run by the Franciscans until the Reformation. In the year 1534, Silken Thomas used the grounds of this church to brief his men for the attack on Dublin Castle. Parts of this Liberty were divided among William Brabazon, Thomas Stephens, William Hande, Thomas Luttrell and J. Seagrave. Stephens later sold all the church property to merchants from England.

Saint Sepulchre's

Laurence O'Toole is dead. A new Archbishop of Dublin has arrived from England. His name is John Comyn and he is the first Anglo-Norman to rule the See. His residence stands beside the priory of the Holy Trinity (Christ Church) and within the civic jurisdiction. A few years later he takes a walk down to the site of St Patrick's Well. After his visit and his prayers, he looks around and finds a suitable site to build his palace, well outside the city wall. The palace of Colonia was soon erected. It transpired that Comyn was given

OLD DUBLIN TOWN

The spire of Saint Patrick's Cathedral looks down on the old Palace of St Sepulchre's, now used as a Garda station.

these lands by King John, though by right they belonged to Christ Church Cathedral.

Comyn now turned his attention to the small church at St Patrick's Well and decided that on this site he would build a new church to God, Our Blessed Lady Mary and St Patrick. This church was solemnly dedicated on St Patrick's Day, 17 March, 1192. Comyn now tried to abolish the cathedral of Christ Church and operate from St Patrick's where he had his own Liberty of Colonia. He failed and that is why we have two cathedrals today. He did gain a charter from the King for his Liberty and later changed the name of his palace and Liberty to that of St (Holy) Sepulchre. Heraclius, the Patriarch of Jerusalem, wrote to Comyn to pray for an increase of interest in the Crusades for the recovery of the Holy Sepulchre from infidel hands. The Liberty became known as the Archbishop's Liberty of St Sepulchre.

The Archbishop's palace is now Kevin Street Garda Station with only the

ME JEWEL AND DARLIN' DUBLIN

gate-posts, a coat of arms and a window as relics of its historic past. The Liberty of St Sepulchre ran as far as Tallaght and Milltown. It included The Coombe and Cork Street and stretched out to South Circular Road into Harold's Cross. Here it was divided from the Liberty of Thomas Court and Donore by the waters of the River Poddle. The Archbishop had his own courts, prisons and gallows and was indeed a very powerful man.

Dean's Liberty

At a later stage a Liberty was granted to the Dean and Chapter of St Patrick's and this was known as the Dean's Liberty. He, too, had his own courts and owned the lands by St Patrick's Park, Bull Alley and Golden Lane. Down the years there have been many disagreements between the Archbishop and the Dean over Liberties and Courts.

Sandwiched between the palace of St Sepulchre (the present Garda station) and St Patrick's is the oldest public library in Ireland. It was founded by Arch-

St Patrick's Close. Left is the Cathedral and in the background is Marsh's Library, both open to the public. Next is the Garda Station and in the right foreground is the Cathedral Grammar School.

bishop Marsh and built in 1701. The beautiful dark oak interior has remained unchanged for nearly three hundred years. Here you will find enough material for a lifetime's study – 25,000 books relating to the 16th, 17th and early part of the 18th centuries. The oldest book in the library is Cicero's 'Letters to his Friends', printed in Milan in 1472. Some of the manuscripts are even older.

Across the road from St Patrick's Cathedral, at 26 Patrick Street, was Emmet's depot and next-door was P. J. McCall's public house. P. J. was a poet and scribe of the Liberties who loved and knew this area like the back of his hand. When is someone going to erect a monument to him in St Patrick's Park? It was around this area that Clarence Mangan wrote his poetry and Dan Donnelly learned boxing. John Field the composer played here as a child and John Austin, the Jesuit who founded Saul Court Academy, went to Dean Swift's school nearby. Jemmy Hope, the United Irishman, often took his wife, Rose, for a walk through these streets.

This is also the district where the Huguenots settled, bringing with them from France their fine skills and traditions. Their word was their bond and the saying 'as honest as a Huguenot' testified to their quality of integrity which fitted like a glove into this area. They were industrious people and built the Weavers' Hall, beautiful houses, shops, schools and churches. They taught the people of Dublin to weave silks, tabinets and Irish poplin, the finest poplin in the world. By their diligence and hard work they set up a hive of industry throughout this part of Dublin, which thrived until England wiped it out because of its effect on her own similar industries, particularly linen and poplin.

The Huguenots also brought us the garden shears, several species of flowers, a florist club and our very first pineapples to Ward's Hill in the Liberties. Many of their graves were in Peter Street Cemetery, which is no longer in existence. The remains in all the graves were removed to Mount Jerome to make way for a car-park for Jacob's biscuit factory. There are also graves in St Stephen's

Green and in the old cabbage garden, which still exists opposite the gates of Kevin Street Garda Station. So let us salute the names of Le Bas, Lefroy, La Touche, Le-Clerc, Le Fanu, Dufour, Ducros, D'Olier, Montfort, Fleury, Boileau, Saurin, Espinasse and Bouhereau, the eminent physician from Rochelle who was the gifted librarian of Marsh's Library.

All religions lived together in the Liberties – Quakers, Jews, Mrs Smylie's Homes, Margaret Aylward's Convent of the Holy Faith, Nano Nagle's schools in Blackpitts, John Wesley on tour and Frank Duff who founded the Legion of Mary in Francis Street. Irish, English, Latin, Dutch, French and Italian were spoken around this area as well as another language the clergy did not know!

Take a walk down the Coombe, down where Jemmy Hope's shop (No.8) used to be, and on to where Margaret Boyle's old Coombe Hospital once stood. It was founded for the poor of Dublin. The old steps and doorway have been preserved. The architect asked me to name all the old street charac-

Gone! Gone forever is the old Coombe Hospital founded by Margaret Boyle in 1826. It was demolished, except for the entrance, in 1974.

ters who would have been born in the old Coombe Hospital. The names are there today, carved into the stone of the steps, including the name of 'Bang Bang', even though he was born in the Rotunda Hospital! Go on to Ardee Street to Con Colbert's outpost in 1916, once Watkins' Brewery. Walk up to St Joseph's Night Shelter which was the old stove tenter house, founded by Thomas Pleasants for the poor weavers of the Liberties to help them dry their cloth in wet weather.

Fr Spratt (Carmelite) born in Cork Street on 5 January, 1796, turned the old empty stove house into a night shelter for poor women and children. It was he who found the ancient statue of Our Lady of Dublin which originally stood in St Mary's Abbey. He also saved the ancient 'lucky stone' which belonged to St Audoen's Church. He was also responsible for getting the site in Whitefriars Street for the Carmelite Church. This site was where the first Carmelite church had stood in the 13th century.

The Lord Mayor's Liberty

The Lord Mayor of Dublin was a bit 'browned-off' or 'fed up' with Liberties. It seemed as if they were closing in on him, so a new term was used when referring to the city inside the walls of Dublin – the Lord Mayor's Liberty. The citizens within had the right of franchise, provided of course that they paid the fine of a pair of gloves to the Lord Mayor's wife. One Lord Mayor admitted so many people to the franchise that his wife was able to open a glove shop in Skinner's Row (Christ Church Place).

A citizen also had the liberty of standing with the 'butter boys' to sell his products in the open markets of the city. The trade guilds were all in the city in the 14th and 15th centuries and had the liberty of fixing the prices for their products. Anyone breaking the rules lost his liberties and ended up in prison or in the common stock on Christ Church Hill. Citizens also enjoyed the protection of the city walls, guarded by the night watch. They could leave

ME JEWEL AND DARLIN' DUBLIN

Looking under the arch of Christ Church and down Winetavern Street towards the River Liffey.

and enter again by the city gates without fear of being stopped by the beadles who manned the gates to keep strangers, swine, dogs and sheep out of the city.

They could also enjoy the voice of the good singing boy and the musicians who were employed by the Lord Mayor to entertain the people in the streets. Now that was an excellent custom: why don't we have today a good ballad group walking around the streets, playing music and singing 'Molly Malone', 'Biddy Mulligan' and 'Twenty men from Dublin town'?

The Lord Mayor and the City Fathers met in the Tholsel at Skinner's Row, beside Ram Alley. On certain days of the year, the Lord Mayor put a complete stop on all liberties and ordered all citizens within and all other people without to come into the city and give a day's work free of charge to mend the pot-holes in the streets. If anyone refused to come, the watch was sent out to drag him in.

The city also had a charter *De Libertate Civitatis Dublini* (For the Freedom of the Citizens of Dublin) from King John granting it lands on the north-side (outside the walls) from St Mary's Abbey to Clonliffe by the Tolka.

The Lord Mayor at one stage ordered all pest-houses (fever hospitals) to be built outside the city walls and a few men to be employed to look after the sick and bury the dead. He also appointed a beadle to carry a forty-foot long white stick and walk in front of the sick on their way to the pest-house. This is where we get the saying, still common today: 'I wouldn't touch him with a forty-foot pole'.

Liberty of Christ Church

Poor Christ Church! Sure they didn't get a look in at all. The bit of land from King John never brought them a halfpenny. And those fellows down the hill in St Patrick's made life a terrible burden for them. Time and again they asked: 'What are we going to do? Everyone has a liberty except us. We are the oldest cathedral (1038). We have right on our side, truth on our side, tradition on our side and the markets on our side' (Fishamble Street). 'That's it,' said the Prior, 'the markets on our land. Why didn't I think of that before?

'Let's go to the Thosel and demand our liberty. Let us pray first. Let us now meditate.' A few hours later they met in Council. 'Well, my brothers, shall we make our demands?' A wise voice answered: 'Why not do it the other way? Let us lobby a few of the City Fathers, get them to make the demand on our behalf.'

'The perfect idea! Who will we approach first?' 'I know an alderman who is a true friend of Christ Church.' At the next meeting of the City Fathers, the question was asked about Christ Church Cathedral.

Soon the gates of Fishamble were joined to the gates of Christ Church and the Prior held the only key. Then a toll was levied to get in or get out. The Manor and Courts of Grangegorman (Manor Street) were started and later still more lands were granted in Phibsborough and Glasnevin. Christ Church had its liberties at last. In fact they did very well indeed. They even had 'Dublin's Hell' and also Winetavern Street with its 137 ale-houses. The Prior hadn't

This was the view of the back of Christ Church Cathedral and St Audoen's Church before the 'redevelopment' of the Wood Quay area.

to go far for a drop in those days.

The Provost of Trinity College, Dublin, told the students on more than one occasion that 'Dublin's hell' was out of bounds and that he would expel anyone found there at night-time. 'Hell' was the site just beyond Christ Church Yard near St Michael's Hill. It was a small area of taverns and bed-and-breakfast establishments in the Monto style. Robert Burns, the poet, wrote a few verses about Dublin's Hell. This place had nothing to do with 'The Four Corners of Hell'. In fact, we really had eight corners of Hell. These were all pubs, the first four being in Longford Street, Ship Street, Stephen's Street and Golden Lane and the second four at Patrick Street, Dean Street, New Street and Kevin Street.

Christ Church Cathedral is worth a visit any day of the week. Go up and have a look at what is claimed to be the tomb of Strongbow and his son, lying side-by-side. Visit the crypt, walk slowly around the chapels, kneel down on a pew, close your eyes and perhaps you will see Lambert Simnel (the impostor) sitting on a throne and on his head the golden crown which was taken from the Virgin's statue in the church of St Maria del Dam. He now claims to be King of Ireland and England (1487), having been proclaimed and crowned by the citizens of Dublin and the clergy of Christ Church Cathedral.

Open your eyes, stand up, look at your pew. Was that the pew that Laurence O'Toole knelt at when he was Archbishop? In the crypt you will find the ancient stocks, a relic of the old Liberties of Christ Church Cathedral.

Clontarf

Clontarf – *Cluain-Tarbh* or plain of the bulls – a fitting name for all the bull the Vernons tried to pull in old Clontarf. In 1014, on Good Friday morning, King Brian fought the Danes and drove them into the sea near Conquer Hill. When the Anglo-Normans came, Hugh de Lacy gave Clontarf to Adam de Phepoe. Adam built Clontarf Castle in 1175. On his death, the castle and lands passed into the hands of the Knights Templar. In 1312, this order was suppressed and all their property passed to the Knights Hospitallers of St John of Jerusalem. When, in turn, this order was suppressed at the Reformation, the castle and lands were given to the Prior John Rawson. He was created Viscount Clontarf, after handing over all the lands and property, including the vast lands covering Kilmainham and the Phoenix Park. When Rawson died, the lands became the property of the King.

After 1649, Clontarf was divided between John Blackwell and John Vernon, followers of Oliver Cromwell. Blackwell later sold his interest to Vernon, who was Quarter-Master-General of Cromwell's army, and who then became lord and master of Clontarf Castle and lands. John Vernon was the grand-nephew of Sir George Vernon of Haddon of Derbyshire, who was known as 'King of the Peak.'

The Vernons continued in possession and in the year 1731 there was a court action between them and the Dublin Corporation over the Liberty of Clontarf Island and the sea. Vernon claimed his Liberty for himself, stating that the City's liberty boundary ended at Clonliffe Road. Cromwell had told the first Vernon that he could own the lands and sea as far as his eye could see, prompting him to claim that he could see Liverpool on a fine day. However, the Vernons lost the court action and this gave Dublin Corporation the green light to move in on the other Liberties. Within 130 years they completed the job.

In the year 1650, the sand island of Clontarf was turned into a pest-house by the Lord Mayor of Dublin. Vernon did not object to this. In fact, it seems he suggested it himself.

For many years, a Captain Cromwell lived in a wooden house on Clontarf Island. His son, Christopher, had a public-house in Beaver Street. After the captain died, his son moved into the island house which was known as Cromwell's Court. On the night of 9 October, 1844, a storm washed the wooden house away and Christopher Cromwell and his son, William, were both drowned.

Dr Carmichael, the eminent Dublin surgeon and founder of the School of Medicine in Peter Street, was drowned at Sutton Creek on 8 June, 1849. He attempted to cross the creek on horseback at low tide from Dollymount to his residence at Sutton. The tomb of Carmichael is in St George's Churchyard, Whitworth Road, a few yards from the tomb of Annie Hutton, the sweetheart of Thomas Osborne Davis. Annie Hutton's favourite place was Clontarf Island.

You can see that the Liberties spread to various parts of the city and county at different times. However, the old area around Christ Church and St Patrick's is the area known today as 'The Liberties'.

OLD DUBLIN TOWN

AROUND ST WERBURGH'S

THE OUTLINES OF COFFINS AND BONES were caught in the beam of the sexton's lamp as we looked around the vaults of this ancient church. The earth was dry and down the passage we walked to the end of the cell-like vault. There on the ground lay the black coffin, with a brass plate inscribed 'Lord Edward Fitzgerald'. This was the new coffin which his grand-daughter had purchased and not the plain brown one that came from the Newgate Jail. We also looked for the remains of James Ware but looked in vain, for Lord Edward's coffin was the only one still intact.

Lord Edward Fitzgerald was buried in St Werburgh's in the dead of night. Only one mourner, his aunt, Lady Louisa Connolly of Castletown House, Celbridge, followed the coffin. However, an old man witnessed the lonely funeral, recognised Lady Louisa and knew that they were the remains of the rebel chief. Later that night, he entered the vaults and found the plain brown coffin and with a rusty nail scraped the initials 'E.F.'. Years later, on his death-

The lovely iron gates of St Werburgh's Church in Werburgh Street.

bed in High Street, he related his story and by so doing made the task of Lord Edward's grand-daughter easy when she came to Dublin to find her grand father's grave. After the arrest of Lord Edward, his wife and children were sent into exile by Dublin Castle and never returned to Dublin.

We came up by the manhole-type entrance, walked around the churchyard and past the grave of Mayor Sirr and then entered the church near the altar. I paused to examine the beautiful wooden pulpit. It was designed by Francis Johnson and carved by a skilled craftsman named Richard Stewart. Then I closely examined the large bell in the centre of the black-and-white tiled aisle. The bell tells its own story and originally came from the church of St Bride. It has the name 'Napper Tandy', the church warden, on it.

Above, on the balcony, hangs the elaborate coat of arms of George III which, along with the pulpit, came from The Chapel Royal in Dublin Castle. The large windows would appear to assist the acoustics when the sweet notes of the organ flow gently in the air. Many fine musicians have recorded for radio in St Werburgh's church. One I know claimed that the acoustics of St Werburgh's were the finest in Dublin.

Castle Street today and the remains of the La Touche Bank beside Dublin Castle.

OLD DUBLIN TOWN

This illustration of about 1840 shows Dublin Castle, and in Castle Street, behind the lamp standard, appears the La Touche Bank – for many years one of the leading banks in Dublin. the Rates Office on the right was previously the Hibernian Bank and before that Newcomens Bank.

The original entrance facing Werburgh Street is not used and in its hallway lies a 16th century Fitzgerald tomb. Also to be seen is an interesting record which tells the price of a muffled funeral bell in days gone by. By far the most striking feature in the hallway are two old wooden hand-pump fire engines. The parish pumps of latter days were similar to the pumps manufactured by John Oats, who lived at the 'Sign of the Boot' in Dame Street. Oats claimed that he could manufacture 'water ingins' as good as any Londoner.

The entrance to the church today is a doorway in Bristol Buildings in Castle Street. The name Bristol is a reminder of the men and women who came from that city to take over Dublin 800 years ago. Castle Street is steeped in history. Here was the birthplace of James Ware, historian and antiquarian, and alongside was the banking house of David de la Touche. Across the street was the house where Conor Maguire and Lord McMahon planned the 1641 Rising. The beautiful Rates Office was originally Newcomen's Bank. Castle Street was also a hub of booksellers and publishers and also writers. Some of the finest books the street ever saw were those from the quills of James Ware and Duald Mac Fírbis. The latter was hired by Ware to translate 'The Register of Clonmacnoise' and other Gaelic manuscripts. On one of his journeys to Sligo he was mysteriously murdered. After Ware's death, his vast library and collection of translations and manuscripts went into the hands of Lord Clarendon. Dean Swift made an attempt to save them for Dublin but failed. The collection changed hands a few times but ended up in the British Museum under the name of the Clarendon Manuscripts.

Dean Swift was born in Hoey's Court nearby and William Penn, the founder of Pennsylvania, lived for a while beside St Werburgh's. Cromwell also stopped here as did many Quakers, Huguenots and the first Dublin Lodge of the Orange Order.

The last wooden house in Dublin stood at the corner of Castle Street, near St Werburgh's Church. The Rev. Nicholas Walsh, who gave many years' service to St Werburgh's, was the man who first brought Gaelic printing-type to Dublin in 1571. Down the street, John Ogilvy founded the first theatre in 1635.

A most frequent visitor to Werburgh Street was Lady Morgan, who passed by the church each evening on her way to the Queen's Head tavern. They say that Lady Morgan started the tradition of bringing porter home in a milk jug. Did your granny ever send you to the pub for porter? Well, if she did, go up to Werburgh Street and you'll see the pub (now the Napper Tandy) where it all started.

St Werburgh's was Lord Edward's favourite church and it is still very much with us, standing in the shadows between the birthplaces of two Dublin poets – Swift and Mangan.

OLD DUBLIN TOWN

FORD OF HURDLES

FROM BUTT BRIDGE AT LIBERTY HALL to Sean Heuston Bridge near the mainline railway station, the River Liffey is spanned by ten bridges. The river divides the city north and south and is a great boon to tourists and strangers. All you have to do is keep to the Liffey Wall on either side, cross any bridge, keep your bearings, make your way back to the Liffey again and you will never get lost in Dublin.

Take a walk from O'Connell Bridge up along the quay. Pass the Ha'penny Bridge or the Metal Bridge, as it is sometimes called. After it was erected in 1816 it was called Wellington Bridge. It got the name Ha'penny Bridge from the toll that had to be paid years ago to cross the Liffey at this spot. Today the bridge leads to the beautiful Irish tweeds' shop and the Sunday morning markets. This was where Hector Grey stood on his wooden throne selling bargains in all kinds of merchandise. Hector was as much a part of Dublin as the Lord Mayor's chain.

Look across Capel Street Bridge and view the beautiful City Hall at the end of Parliament Street. It was originally designed and opened as a Royal Exchange and it is hard to credit that this was the site of public whipping and garrotting up to the year 1815. Behind City Hall stands Dublin Castle, the only castle in the world that doesn't look like a castle though the State Apartments and the Chapel Royal are worthy of your attention. This was the seat of British power in Ireland for nearly 800 years. Beyond Capel Street Bridge lies Winetavern Street Bridge and beyond that again is Church Street Bridge. Beyond Grattan Bridge at Capel Street lies O'Donovan Rossa's Bridge at Winetavern Street and beyond that again is Father Mathew Bridge, (the old Ford of the Hurdles).

Wait! Stop! Go no further. Stand on Church Street Bridge, look in any direction, stand and think. You are walking in the footprints of St Patrick. Nay, you are walking in the even earlier footprints of The Donn of Cooley.

ME JEWEL AND DARLIN' DUBLIN

You are walking, too, in the footprints of Little John – no, not the one who got out of Mountjoy but his precursor. He was Robin Hood's friend, who came to Dublin from Sherwood Forest and shot an arrow from this bridge to the top of Church Street to show his skill with the bow. Little John was hanged in the fields of Oxmantown beyond the Blue Coat School on the road to Arbour Hill.

Church Street Bridge is at the Ford of Hurdles, the first bridge built across the Liffey and the spot where Dublin gets one of its three Gaelic names, *Baile Átha Cliath* (Ford of Hurdles), *Dubhlinne* (dark river pool), *Druim Cuill Coille* (hazelwood ridge). Church Street Bridge, the Ford of Hurdles, was re-named Fr Mathew Bridge after the great Capuchin temperance priest.

I mentioned there The Donn of Cooley (from *The Táin*). The Donn was the great brown Ulster bull defended by Cúchulain. Now I don't want to go into mythology but we in Dublin (meself and me brother) believe that the bull came from the little green field beside Paddy Ennis's pig-yard in the Liberties. Among other things, the Ford of Hurdles, made of bundles of brushwood laid across the river, enabled the Ulster cattle raiders to get the herds across to the northern road. One of the five great roads from Tara crossed the Liffey at this spot. It was here around 448 that St Patrick is reputed to have said that Dublin would grow to become the principal city of Ireland. So, to honour our 'four green fields', the four provinces of Ireland – Ulster, Munster, Leinster and Connaught – make four short tours from the Ford of Hurdles. And remember, if you get lost, all you have to do is find your way back to the Liffey.

Tour One – Bridge Street

Stand on Church Street Bridge. Facing the city on your left is Church Street and on your right is Lr. Bridge Street. Take Bridge Street first. The vacant site on the corner was once the Dublin home of Rory O'Moore, leader of the 1641 Rising. 'For God, Ireland and Rory O'Moore' was the battle-cry in those days. A later member of the same family founded the Irish College in Rome, became chancellor of a few French universities and was the only non-Frenchman to be given the honour of delivering the commemoration address to celebrate the reign of Louis XIV. Still on vacant ground, on your left was the birthplace of Jimmy O'Dea. The Merchant Bar covers part of James Mullet's tavern where the Invincibles used to meet. It is now one of the best places in Dublin for Irish music and set-dancing. Mullet was chairman of the Irish National Invincibles in 1882 and spent about twelve years of his life in jail. Just beyond the Merchant Bar is a wall on which there used to be a plaque commmorating it as part of the home of Oliver Bond. In fact, there was some confusion about this and the Merchant Bar stands now on the real site. It was here that the Leinster Directory were arrested by Major Sirr on 12 March 1798. The password for the meeting was betrayed to Dublin Castle by Thomas Reynolds who was a member of the Directory. Major Sirr and his men knocked on the door. A voice answered, 'Who's there?' The Major shouted: 'Is Ivers from Carlow come?' The door opened, arrests followed and that evening the Leinster Directory (except for Lord Edward Fitzgerald) were in chains in Newgate Jail.

Oliver Bond was later murdered in the prison yard at Newgate Jail. Across the road from Bond's house is a small laneway which leads to the Brazen Head, the oldest tavern in Ireland – its sign says 1191. It could be said that revolution kept it in business and nearly put it out of business down the years. It was a meeting-place for Irish revolutionaries in 1798, 1803 (see Emmet's desk), 1848, 1867, 1916 and in the Black-and-Tan days. After every rising it was raided. In 1916 it was almost destroyed and in 1922, when the Free State forces shelled the Four Courts garrison, the vibration of the heavy British artillery used shook it to the foundations.

At the top of Lr Bridge Street stood the old Wormwood Gate and the steep hill straight ahead leads to Cornmarket, the birthplace of Napper Tandy (United Irishman). The famous ballad, 'The Wearin' of the Green', has the following verse:

> I met with Napper Tandy and he took me by the hand
> And said 'How's poor old Ireland and how does she stand?
> She's the most distressful country that ever yet was seen
> For they're hangin' men and women for the wearin' of the green.'

Tandy's house at 21 Cornmarket was standing a few years ago, just around the corner on the left, at the top of the hill in High Street. If you look across the road you will see the site of the first Newgate Jail and part of the old town wall which has been preserved. A few years ago the wall, with a gate entrance, ran the length of Lamb Alley. Standing at the wall you can see The Tailors' Hall,

The entrance gate to the Tailors' Hall.

OLD DUBLIN TOWN

The Tailors' Hall, Back Lane, Dublin.

another treasure of Dublin, Francis Street, Mother Redcap's Market and the Iveagh Market. Before you make your way back to the Ford of hurdles for the second tour take a good view of the green domes and the northern skyline.

Tour Two – Oxmantown and Dr Steeven's

This tour takes us along the quays towards the Phoenix Park. Number 12 Arran Quay was the birthplace of Edmund Burke, the golden orator whose statue stands outside Trinity College. And at Number 39 stands the Boss Croker tavern, which has a great collection of racing treasures, including one of Orby's hooves which has been made into an ink-well. Orby, of course, was the first Catholic Irish horse to win both the English and Irish Derbys. Charles Halliday, author of 'Scandinavian Kingdom of Dublin', had offices in Number 27. St Paul's Church, also on Arran Quay, is very popular with Dublin people. It has a beautiful dome and pillars and was one of the first churches to ring out its peal of bells when Catholic Emancipation was granted in 1829.

ME JEWEL AND DARLIN' DUBLIN

After this date a number of Italian marble workers came to Dublin to adorn Catholic churches. Among these craftsmen was a man named Carsoni. His son became an architect and designed St Peter's Church in Phibsborough. Carsoni's grandson was born in Harcourt Street and he, too, was named Edward, after his father. He was educated in Trinity College and in 1900 became Sir Edward Henry. He was M.P. for Dublin University (Trinity) and a Bencher of the King's Inn, Dublin. He helped found Carson's volunteers to fight against Home Rule, and he also worked to establish the Six County Parliament at Stormont.

The next bridge at Queen Street, called Liam Mellows Bridge, leads to the Hay Market and to where Coopers, the horse dealers, used to be and on to Thundercut Alley and the streets to Grangegorman. The turn on your right after Liam Mellows Bridge leads to the old Blue Coat School buildings and the road to Arbour Hill where you will find the graves of the executed leaders of the 1916 Easter Week Rising.

The Blue Coat School was designed by a Corkman, Thomas Ivory, who left us a few gems of Georgian buildings in Dublin. The school got its name from the strange dress of its pupils. The schoolboys wore dark blue cut-away coats with brass buttons, yellow waistcoats, dark blue knee-breeches, yellow stockings and silver buckle shoes. They must have made a colourful sight on the streets of Dublin. Down the times the uniform changed in style but never in colour and, even when the school governors decided to do away with the uniform in 1923, they replaced it with a blue serge suit.

The old Blue Coat building, 'The Hospital and Free School of King Charles II' at Oxmantown, commonly called King's Hospital or Blue Coats, was first founded in 1669 in Queen Street by the Dublin Corporation. A year later, King Charles II granted them a Royal Charter. The Queen Street schoolhouse was once used by the Irish parliament in 1729. The school in Blackhall Place dates from 1784. The new King's Hospital School is at Brooklawn in Palmerstown. A merger has taken place betweeen Morgan House Junior School, Mercers' Girls' School and The King's Hospital.

As you continue up the quay beyond Blackhall Place, you come into 'truck driver country'. This is where a large number of country truck drivers used to 'drum up' (get their meals) before heading into or out of Dublin. Further up along the quays, there stood the Bark Kitchen public-house, where the best ballads in Dublin city were sung every night. Further up still is Ryan's beautiful Victorian Bar at Parkgate Street. The area is noted for a number of neat and tidy and reasonably-priced restaurants and cafes. If it's a ball of malt or a few pints you need, well, there are plenty to choose from.

As you reach Sarsfield Quay, stop and look through the railings. Yes, I know it's a shame with sheep grazing and football pitches on the graves of our heroic dead. This is the 'Croppies' Hole'. What was it that Dr Madden, author of *Lives and Times of United Irishmen*, said? Oh, yes: 'Someday this land will be consecrated and men and women will come with funeral trophies in honour of the noble dead of 1798.' Today, a granite cross marks the spot where Lawless, Esmonde, Teeling, Tone (Matthew, a brother of Wolfe Tone) and countless other forgotten patriots lie in a mass grave.

Collins Barracks in the high background was the old Royal Barracks, the first built in Dublin, where Kipling was inspired to write his Barrack Room Ballad. At the rear of the barracks was the old Provost Prison where Wolfe Tone was murdered in 1798. Cross over the next bridge (Sean Heuston) and, as you do so, note the fine structure on your right. It is the headquarters of CIE, the national transport system, standing in front of the station. Now that the nurses' home has been knocked down, if you look straight ahead you will have a beautiful view of Dr Steeven's Hospital. It dates from 1720 and is the second oldest in Dublin. The hospital courtyard is most unusual and is well worth a visit. As a tribute to all the great hospitals of Dublin, and to the dedicated service of doctors, nurses and staff, I would like to record the name of the late Dr Oliver Chance, one of the greatest skin specialists of Europe, who attended the poor of Dublin for many years in Dr Steeven's and other city hospitals. In the year 1936, on Mondays, Wednesdays and Fridays, he manned the out-patients' dispensary with kindness, courtesy and, above all, dignity. You paid your shilling (five pence in today's money) on a Friday and, if you could not pay, the lady almoner (treasurer) just smiled and told you not to worry about it.

Above the hill from the hospital gate stands Dean Swift's (now St Patrick's) Hospital. Visitors are welcome to visit the Swift Museum in the entrance hall. Then, you had better go back to the bridge on the Liffey. I don't want you to get lost at Bow Lane, the Forty Steps or the Robbers' Den. As you walk down the south side of the Liffey you will pass Guinness's Brewery on your right. The old jetty on the riverside is gone. Sure the Liffey isn't the same at all, at all, since they took down the jetty and got rid of the barges.

The bridge at the corner of Watling Street was known in olden days as Bloody Bridge. No, it had nothing to do with Ireland's fight for freedom but with the fight for freedom of the Liffey. This was a ferry crossing and, when the bridge was built, the ferrymen caused a riot because, as they said, it was, 'taking the bread out of our mouths'. Beyond the bridge is Usher's Island. Number 20 is long gone. It was the home of Francis Magan, the man who informed on Lord Edward Fitzgerald. This did not come to light until several years after Magan's death. However, his sister, Mary, knew that he was the informer. It nearly drove her insane and she never left the house, living the life of a recluse for over forty years. Some historians have stated that it was Mary Magan's life that inspired Charles Dickens to write his book *Great Expectations*.

Only the gate-posts remain of The Mendicity Institution. It was once Moira House, the home of Lord and Lady Moira, and was described by John Wesley as 'the most beautiful house in Europe'. Here Lord Edward Fitzgerald's family lived before being deported to England after his death in Newgate jail in 1798. The house became The Mendicity Institution for paupers in 1828. In 1916, it was an outpost of the G.P.O. garrison, under the command of Sean Heuston, who was later executed. In his last letter to his sister, a Dominican nun, Heuston wrote: 'If you really love me, teach the children the history of Ireland.'

Usher's Island leads onto Usher's Quay. Numbers 18 to 20, where Ganley's the auctioneers had their offices, is now occupied by the Civil Service Union. The premises cover the site where the Quakers lived in their community circle in the last century. The Quakers, like the Huguenots, were always noted for their honest dealings. Their old meeting-house at Number 6 Eustace Street is now the Irish Film Centre. The history of this noble community in Dublin would justify close study.

Tour Three – The Bridewell and St Michan's

As you cross the Ford of Hurdles Bridge, straight ahead is Church Street. The Four Courts Hotel, which closed in 1974, was once the old Angel Inn, dating back to the late 17th century. The first turn on the left is Hammond Lane, the name being a corruption of Hangman's Lane. In the 16th century, this lane led to the common hanging grounds of Oxmantown Woods. The first turn on the right leads to the Bridewell cells and old Pill Lane (Chancery Street). Visitors are not welcome in the Bridewell unless, of course, you have a prior reservation. If that be the case, you will check in at the desk, give your name and address, leave all your luggage, razor-blades, shoe-laces etc. in the cloakroom and climb the stone stairway to your private room, a filthy hole, a hair mattress bed in lumps like the Three Rock Mountains and Kippure, a brown-stained wall around a corner open stone toilet bowl, two dirty blankets and a dirty pillow filled with rocks, I think.

Remember what Oliver St John Gogarty said about Joyce's book *Ulysses*?

ME JEWEL AND DARLIN' DUBLIN

The backyard of the Bridewell and the tower of St Michan's Church.

Well, if Gogarty had ever been in the Bridewell, he would have said that Joyce wrote it here. The cell walls tell their own story: 'Johnny loves Mary': names, dates, sex talk, football teams, 'Up Bohs', 'Shag Rovers'; threats to the judge, the fuzz, the cops; poems, dirty jokes, the Red Flag Chairman Mao, noughts and crosses.

'I'll never steal again. I'm very sorry. No, I'll never steal again,' under which was written: 'Cut out the bloody moaning and do your time ... and make sure they don't catch you next time out'; 'Good luck, Joey and Mona,' and 'Frankie Reilly slept here'. During the night, you get out of bed a few times for a rest. The toilet chain is outside the cell door, in case you hang yourself with it. In the morning the charlady shouts in the spy-hole: 'Son, son, do you want your chain pulled? Son, will I pull your chain, son?' Lately the Bridewell have gone all modern but only in relation to the toilet chain. Everything else remains the same but the charlady is missing and a computer press-button system in a downstairs office flushes all the cell toilets in one go.

The street outside the Bridewell door leads to the old Pill Lane and it may be of interest to the Dublin branch of Women's Lib that, as far back as 1641, King Charles I signed and sealed a Royal Charter granting the 'pill' to all citizens of Dublin. The charter also said that the pill was for their childer and their childers' childer for ever and ever, Amen. In fact, the pill was the name of a miniature harbour used by St Mary's Abbey and various traders over the centuries. This was years before the Liffey quay walls were built.

Millar's Dublin Copper and Brass Works was a long-established company, part of its premises in Church Street covering the site of the house of Henry Jackson, one of the United Irishmen, who had an iron foundry here in 1776. His daughter, Eleanor, born at this spot, became the wife of Oliver Bond. Eleanor was also a member of the United Irishmen and administered the organisation's oath to several distinguished Dublin recruits. After Oliver

Bond's death, Eleanor and the children emigrated to America, returning to Dublin about the year 1820 to unveil a statue to her father. She herself lived to a ripe old age and is buried in Boston, Mass.

Across the road stands St Michan's Church, pronounced by Dubliners as 'Saint Mick-ann's'. Founded in 1095, this church is steeped in history. Go in and visit the vaults and graveyard. See the baptismal font where the waters were poured on the heads of Eleanor Bond and Edmund Burke. Sit on the stool of repentance, the only one in Dublin. Note the pulpit, the altar rail, the fine wood carving on the front of the organ gallery. This was Parnell's favourite Dublin church. If you hear the organ playing and yet see no one at it, it might be the ghost of Handel back again to play another tune before going to the Fishamble Street Music Hall in April 1742 to perform for the first time his famous *Messiah*.

The vaults of St Michan's contain the coffins of the Sheares brothers who died side by side on the scaffold outside Newgate jail in 1798. In the graveyard seek out the graves of Oliver Bond, Dr Charles Lucas and the Rev. Mr Jackson. Place a flower on their clay, for these three men loved Ireland and should always be remembered and honoured.

Your next stop as you walk up Church Street must be the Capuchin Friary. The first names that spring to mind are Albert and Dominick, Columbus, Sebastian, Aloysius and Augustine – all friars who were deeply involved in the Irish struggle for freedom from 1916 to 1923. Many books could be filled with the stories of their deeds, from the bullet-swept streets of Dublin with Elizabeth O'Farrell and Pearse's surrender order, to the execution yard in Kilmainham Jail and to exile and pain in far-off lands. Both Fr Albert Bibby and Fr Dominick O'Connor were sent into exile in 1924. Within ten months, Fr Albert was dead. His dying request was that his body should rest on Irish soil: 'Let me rest with Liam, Rory and the boys in Glasnevin.' He died on 14 February 1925, in Santa Barbara, California.

OLD DUBLIN TOWN

Beyond the Capuchin Friary is the Father Mathew Hall where the annual Father Mathew Feis is held. Here the little children of Dublin dance and sing, recite, act and speak verse in competition for silver cups and medals. At the cross-roads was Reilly's Fort, an outpost of the 1916 Rising. On the far side of the road, in front of the new flats, Kevin Barry was arrested in 1920. As you walk up the hill, the first turn on your left leads to the old Channell Row convent site. This convent was founded by the Benedictine sisters in 1689. They were expelled the following year. Then the Poor Clare sisters moved in, but they too were expelled. In 1717, six foundresses of the Dominican Order moved into the same convent. They were Mary Bellew, Julia Brown, Ellen Keating, Alice Rice, Elizabeth Weaver and Honora Vaughan. In 1819 the sisters moved to their present site at Cabra and are continuing in the same tradition that started in Channell Row.

The front of the former Richmond Hospital in North Brunswick Street.

ME JEWEL AND DARLIN' DUBLIN

The fine building running along North Brunswick Street with the many small green domes was the main front of the Richmond Hospital. It was joined to the Hardwicke and Whitworth Hospitals. Unfortunately, the buildings are no longer in use as hospitals. Some have been demolished and the rest refurbished for alternative use. The three hospitals were known as the House of Industry Hospitals and covered the land of the ancient House of Industry, later known as the North Dublin Union. This was the first workhouse built in Dublin in the late 17th century.

Near the top of Constitution Hill is the old Broadstone railway station, now a bus depot. Across the road behind the high iron railings is the large impressive building known as The King's Inns. The present building dates from 1800 and covers part of Lord Mountjoy's land (that man again!). The area was once known as Primate's Hill and leads to Henrietta Street by a small arch-type gateway at the rear of a building where Lord Mountjoy had one of his town houses. The King's Inn library was erected in 1827 at a cost of £20,000 and contained over 100,000 volumes of books dealing with legal and historical matters and a wide range of books on Dublin's history. It seems that The King's Benchers were more concerned with eating food than drinking knowledge, as their dining-hall cost £34,000 and since 1822 considerable sums have been spent on repairs and decorations. In 1973, the Benchers sold by auction in London many priceless books from the library. Some of these were rescued by An Taisce, which bought at the auction various rare items relating to Ireland.

During the 1798 Rising, five members of The King's Inns were 'struck from the rolls forever' for the part they played in the ranks of the United Irishmen. On your way back down the hill to the Ford of Hurdles for the fourth and final tour, watch out for a horseman riding fast. It may be King James running away from the Battle of the Boyne in 1690. When he reached Dublin Castle, he complained: 'The cowardly Irish ran away and left me.'

The lady at the Castle gate quickly retorted: 'It seems that Your Majesty has won the race.'

Tour Four – Merchant's Quay and the Four Courts

This tour starts across The Ford of Hurdles and down Merchant's Quay. On the far side of the Liffey stands Gandon's and Cooley's Four Courts. This is the best spot from which to admire the fine building with its green dome and bullet-scarred pillars. The scars date from 28 June 1922, and recall the Civil War and Rory O'Connor, Liam Mellows, Dick Barrett and Joe McKelvey of

Henrietta Street showing the back entrance to The King's Inns. To the left is the Law Library.

the Republican forces. They recall, too, the scribbled note from Fr Albert Bibby O.F.M. Cap.: 'I was hearing confessions from 1 a.m. to 11 p.m., non-stop.' Fr Albert's mind must have flashed back to the execution yard in Kilmainham Jail as he stood a few paces from Sean Heuston in 1916, and to the scaffold in Mountjoy Jail as he stood beside Kevin Barry in November 1920; or perhaps he wondered whose grave or whose execution would be next. Within ten days it will be Cathal Brugha's grave in Glasnevin. Within four months he will be denied a last visit with Erskine Childers. Rory O'Connor, Liam Mellows, Dick Barrett and Joe McKelvey were taken prisoners at the Four Courts and were to die as a Free State reprisal on 8 December, 1922.

The Four Courts stand on ancient lands where the Dominican Friars built their Abbey in the year 1224, three years after the death of St Dominick. For many years they had a toll chapel on The Ford of Hurdles. The history of the Dominicans in Dublin is a long and chequered one. In 1539, the prior of St Saviour's, Patrick Hay, surrendered the monastery to King Henry VIII. Three years later, the lands were handed over to the Chancellor, John Allen, the Lord Chief Justice and other professors of law.

The Inns of Court were established and here the Benchers had their rooms, meals and books until they moved to The King's Inns. The Four Courts remained and what are they called – The District? The Circuit? The Supreme? The High? The building contains, in fact, the Courts of Chancery, King's Bench, Common Pleas and Exchequer – and if you are caught with no light on your bike you could end up in one of them. Of course, these terms are not used today and there are now eleven courts within the 'Four Courts' complex.

As you turn your eyes back to Merchant's Quay, remember that in the attack on the Four Courts in 1922, the Records Office was completely destroyed by fire. This office contained several rare documents and manuscripts, relating to the early history of Dublin and Ireland. It also contained the early records of St Michan's Church and many other parishes which had been transferred to

OLD DUBLIN TOWN

The Four Courts for safety.

Merchant's Quay gets its name from the hive of merchants, many of whom had their own vessels two hundred years ago. In fact, up to about fifty years ago, the side entrance to Adam and Eve's church was known as Skippers' Alley. It would appear that this alley was reserved for the skippers and masters of the many vessels, native and foreign, that sailed up the Liffey's waters.

Adam and Eve's Church (the Franciscan Friary) gets its name from the old Adam and Eve's Tavern which was used as a Mass-house during the penal days. The two St Anthony's Halls beside the church are noted for concerts, carpet sales and bingo games. The Church has a fine theatre, bookshop and repository. If you walk down the park between the church and hall, it will lead you out to Cook Street, the street of the cooks, which was noted for good food, taverns by the score and churches by the half-dozen. It once held five Order churches and many Mass-houses. This was also for the hub of the printing industry in Dublin and they were fond of using colourful names such as The Sign of the Bible, The Sign of the Angel, The Sign of Dr Hay's Head (Bridge Street corner).

Conor Maguire and Lord McMahon were arrested in 1641 where the modern schools stand today. They were later executed in Tyburn, England. Facing the school is the true gem of Dublin, the only remaining gateway in the old city walls – St Audoen's Arch. It was one of the first gates erected in the Danish stronghold of Dublin after the Battle of Clontarf in 1014. Only part of the old city wall remains. Climb the steps slowly and listen. This is the spot where you can feel the heart of old Dublin. Don't rush, take your time. You are in footprints of Ailred the Dane, going home to Newgate to start his hospital, and the noble tradition of the Augustinian Order in old John's Lane.

St Audoen's Church is a 'must' for a visit. Three of its six bells are dated 1423 and are the oldest in Ireland. Call in and see the silver plate, touch the lucky or blessed stone in the hallway and sense the spirits of hundreds and

ME JEWEL AND DARLIN' DUBLIN

*The Four Courts and Winetavern Street
(now O'Donovan Rossa) Bridge viewed from Wood Quay.*

hundreds of years of history. The top of the steps leads to High Street, or Main Street, Dublin, which dates back to the year A.D.120 when Conn of the Hundred Battles and King Mogh of Munster divided Ireland between them and made High Street the border-line of the two kingdoms.

Turn to your left, walk down to the new St Audoen's Church and then Christ Church Cathedral. You will pass the site of the house where Wolfe Tone's body was waked in 1798. The Cathedral dates from 1038 and its history is long and colourful. Go down under the archway of Christ Church into Winetavern Street and you will find yourself back at the Liffey wall. On your right are the new Dublin Corporation offices built over the foundations of a Viking settlement. Breandán Ó Ríordáin and his team from the National Museum found priceless treasures of Viking days, dating back to the 9th century, on this site. Despite many protest marches, sit-ins and objections by the vast majority of Dublin's citizens, the Corporation still went ahead and built two of the most ugly monstrosities here. I've yet to meet a person who likes them! Further on lies St Michael's and John's Church, which has been deconsecrated and is to become a Viking Museum.

Across the way is Fishamble Street Music Hall where Handel first performed his *Messiah* on 13 April, 1742. The rear of the church stands where the old Smock Alley Theatre stood and it was here that Peg Woffington made her name as she performed in the *Beggar's Opera*. During the interval, Peg came out into the street to help her mother sell apples and oranges to the crowd from the gallery and the pit.

St Audoen's Church.

St James's Gate, the main entrance to Guinness's Brewery. The house on the left, No. 1 Thomas Street, is where the 'first Arthur' lived after he bought the brewery.

CHAPTER 4

Commercial Life

BACK OF THE PIPES

'Where are we going to hide our school-bags?' 'What about the Robbers' Den or the tunnels in the Brickfields?' 'No, the last time we hid them there we couldn't remember which tunnel we put them in.' 'How about the back of the pipes?' We were on the mitch from school so off we went down to the back of the pipes to hide our bags.

The same question was asked by the City Fathers in 1638. 'How about the back of the pipes?' 'Well, what about them?' 'They are leaking, these pipes, I mean.' 'What do you want me to do?' 'You're the Lord Mayor, you decide.' 'But the people will soon have no water.' The Lord Mayor decided: 'Send a man to London for five tons of lead and a plumber.'

Three weeks later the lead and two plumbers arrived. The work started at the back of the pipes on a site of land known as Lowsie Hill, pronounced *Lousy Hill* by Dubliners. The plumbers repaired the pipes and advised the Corpo that yer man at the top of Lowsie Hill, the brewer named Giles Mee, had too much of a draw off the city pipes and if he didn't look after the back of the pipes the city would have no water. Mee, who was also a city Alderman, did not want to lose his brewery, so he looked after the back of the pipes.

ME JEWEL AND DARLIN' DUBLIN

After his death the brewery was given to his son-in-law, another Alderman, and later Lord Mayor of Dublin, Sir Mark Rainsford. He, too, left his name on one of our streets. He even opened up a theatre on Lowsie Hill but it was a flop as the people of Dublin said it was too far out of the city.

The brewery was now being run by Rainsford's son, also named Mark, and in 1750 he rented it to a Huguenot named Paul Espinasse, who was later killed by a fall off his horse near the Black Bull Inn at Drogheda.

The Corpo had the brewery for a while and a couple of others tried to keep it going over the years. About this time, Arthur Guinness was in Wales looking for a suitable place to start a brewery. Thanks be to God, he couldn't find one. He came home to Dublin and went for a walk up to the back of the pipes. He saw the empty brewery on Lowsie Hill, found the owner, Mark Rainsford, and in 1759 did a deal and got the lot, lock stock and barrel, for a lease of 9,000 years at a rent of £45 a year. Isn't it a nice thought to know that you'll be able to drink Guinness for the next 8765 years?

If I can take a liberty to say it, Dublin is a great city for drink and religion. You'll never run short of a pub or a church in Dublin. We have two-and-a-half Cathedrals and wasn't someone going to build another one at Merrion Square? Now I hear we are going to get another half-Cathedral in Westland Row. It was Roe's whiskey that put the roof on Christ Church and Guinness's porter that restored St Patrick's Cathedral in 1974/5 for the city and the nation.

Sure, don't drink and religion go hand in hand? Christ's first miracle didn't change the water into lemonade! No, it was wine and a good drop too, I believe. And didn't St Patrick have his chief brewer, Mescan, by his side when he came to Dublin in 448? In the year 1610 we had 91 breweries and 1180 ale-houses and 39 chapels and churches in Dublin.

It was the Archbishop of Cashel, Dr Price, who started Arthur Guinness at

COMMERCIAL LIFE

beer-making. Arthur's father was an estate agent for the Bishop and he often made a few buckets of table beer. The Bishop liked his drop and soon learned that young Arthur made a superior bucket of brew. The praise went to young Arthur's head and as soon as he grew up he started the business.

The waters for Guinness come from a spring in County Kildare named St James's Well. Another well under Guinness's is used for cooling purposes. Remember the recipe – malt, hops, yeast and water – and you, too, might build the largest brewery in the world. But until that day comes, you can still see one of the wonders of the world, the brewery of Arthur Guinness standing on Lowsie Hill at the back of the pipes. The pipes came along by Dolphin's Barn, down the laneway beside Maryland and the canal (where we hid our school-bags), around by the canal and out into Thomas Street via Crane Street.

Within a stone's throw of the pipes was Marrowbone Distillery where Ceannt and McDonagh had a meeting before they decided on surrender in 1916. Marrowbone Lane was an outpost to the South Dublin Union garrison, which was just across the canal. Marrowbone Lane also has the distinction of being the place where Charles Cameron started his free sulphur depot for the poor of Dublin. Cameron was the city's Medical Officer and made many changes during his long term with the Dublin Corporation. Sulphur was an expensive product, which only the rich could buy in time of fever. A sulphur bath, hot or cold, was three shillings, which was equal to three weeks' pay for a labourer in those dark Victorian days. Sulphur and the free disinfecting systems soon checked the outbreak of fevers in Dublin.

If you ask a religious Dubliner how to get from Dame Street to the back of the pipes, the answer will be: 'Go up by Christ Church, don't turn the hill to St Patrick's, keep on by the new St Audoen's Church and the old St Audoen's

Church, go on by John's Lane Church to St Catherine's and turn left before you come to St James's Church. You can't miss St James's, it's nearly facing the other St James's Church on the far side. Ah, sure, you're welcome and God bless ye.'

If you ask a drinking man the same question, the answer will be: 'Go up past the Stag's Head, don't turn the corner to the Long Hall. Go on by the City Hall Inn, past the Oak, up by the Castle and the Lord Edward. Don't go down the hill to the Brazen Head and the Merchant, but on up by Ryan's clock and take the first turn on your left after you pass O'Reilly's pub. That, sir, will take you to the back of the pipes. You're welcome, sir, and they all shut at eleven!'

Henry Grattan once said that he regarded the brewery at the back of the pipes (Guinness's) as 'the actual nurse of the people and entitled to every encouragement, favour, and exemption'. Maybe we could look for a liberty to take tax off porter because, after all, porter first saw the light of day in Dublin's first Liberty in the Abbot's garden at the back of the pipes.

MERCHANTS AND MARKETS

'OCTOBER 1870. Mr and Mrs A. Cameron, 73 Grafton Street, Dublin, beg to announce their return from the markets and the arrival of their new goods, the latest fashions in millinery, mantles and dress materials, and call particular attention to a lot of sealskin mantles and black and coloured silks purchased considerably under price.'

I doubt very much if the Camerons, when they published this notice, had been to the Daisy Market, the Iveagh, Norfolk or Patrick Street markets or, for that matter, to the Phoenix Park Market, Mother Redcap's, Johnny Giles's Markets or the Meath Street Liberties Markets. Dublin City has always been

COMMERCIAL LIFE

a great centre for markets, merchants and traders of all kinds. It would be impossible to list all the interesting ones, so you'll forgive me if I only pick a select few.

The firm of John G. Rathborne Ltd., East Wall Road, Dublin 3, is the oldest firm in Dublin. The family claims to have come to Dublin from Chester in the year 1488 but I would like to think that the Rathbornes were in Ireland centuries before and that possibly some of them were in Dublin when the foundation stone of St Werburgh's Church was laid in the 13th century. In Chester today stands the Cathedral which was at one time the Abbey of St Werburgh. So it is most likely that the men of Chester had some influence in having a church in Dublin bearing the name Werburgh.

The firm of Rathborne's are 'Manufacturers in Wax and Spermaceti Candles'. In the mid-13th century, candle-making was confined to rich and private houses, many of which used beeswax from their honey hives. Mutton fat was also an expensive product. The poor used rush-lights. By their method of manufacturing candles, the Rathbornes made them available to the poor as well as to the rich. How many times have you heard the expression: 'You could not hold a candle to it,' meaning that something is beautiful or the very best. This expression gives a fair idea of the high esteem in which candles were held.

The Rathbornes started business inside the old city walls near St Werburgh's Church. Down the centuries they moved to several different locations, including St Mary's Abbey, Stoneybatter, Parnell Street, East Wall and Essex Street. It seems that in each generation the family changed premises. A letter in the firm's files today reveals that, at one time in the 1840s, the company was a little short of capital and this was provided on loan by Rev. Thos. Luby, D.D., a Fellow of Trinity College, who was married to Jane Rathborne. For special reasons, church candles are still made of beeswax in the same fashion as they were centuries ago.

I don't think there is a house or room in Dublin which hasn't got a candle or maybe a half-a-candle. The next time the lights fail and you search for your spare candle, remember John Rathborne, the man who brought candles within the reach of the poor of Dublin for centuries.

One of the greatest merchants Dublin ever had was Daniel Maguire, who had his own Rope Manufacturing Company in Blackpitts in the Liberties about 1798. He exported his products to Germany, Russia and Poland in his own vessels. This historic fact would never have been known but for his letter in 1803 to Major Sirr, telling about his sixteen-year-old son, who was a prisoner in the Provost jail. The original letter is in the Sirr collection of papers and letters in Trinity College. Daniel Maguire lived beside his rope works on the site of ground known as 'Ropers' Rest', a favourite haunt of Robert Emmet. He also had a house in Francis Street.

Goodbody's cigarette factory in Granville Place was the first tobacco factory in Dublin. Mr Goodbody moved from Tullamore, Co. Offaly to Blackpitts. At one time he grew his own tobacco and had over two hundred girls employed hand-rolling cigarettes.

Dolphin's Barn Brick Works was another old firm. It was situated at the first lock on the Grand Canal. Its rival was Hunter's of Corporation Street, which sold Newry bricks. William Hunter sold these bricks all over Dublin and Ireland. Hunter's proudly advertised the quality of their product as follows:

'Granite Sand, carried down the streams from the Mourne mountains, forms the main portion of the material from which our Bricks are made, and anyone with a rudimentary knowledge of chemistry knows this is an almost indestructible substance by either heat, cold, acids, or alkalies. It is fused

COMMERCIAL LIFE

by the action of intense heat and chemical action of lime, etc., into a Solid Pressed and Panelled and Facing Brick.'

How could you beat that? Sure, it's no wonder The Dolphin Brick Works closed down.

Telford and Telford were the organ-builders who supplied organs to dozens of churches and cathedrals in Ireland. It was Telford's who found the mummified remains of a cat and mouse in the organ of Christ Church Cathedral. You can see them both today in the crypt of Christ Church.

The Dublin Pure Ice Company did a roaring trade before the electric fridge was invented. The ice-lollies of today are nothing compared to a silver lump of pure Dublin ice.

The charcoal-makers were in Cuffe Lane, headed by Daniel Mahar. Do you remember the charcoal-driven motor-vans during the last war or was your car the type with the large gas balloon on the roof? The charcoal vans were great for a heat in the winter days or for lighting your cigarette to save a match.

Many old family firms which were household names to Dubliners have gone while quite a few old names are still with us, although in many cases only the name is there and the old business is now part of a large group. Pidgeon's, Stein's, Stump's, Youkstetterr's and May Clarke were best for sausages, black and white pudding and pigs' feet. Hafner's made quality sausages for years but they were taken over years ago by H. Williams. Once you could go to Ruddle's, Taylor's and Lundy Foot of Parliament Street for your snuff. Other Dublin companies of renown were Kelly's Cigars in Camden Street, the Irish Tobacco Company on Merchant's Quay and the Dublin Japan Works in Jervis Street. These last were expert japanners, enamellers and platers. Devlin's of Francis Street made clay pipes. You can still go to Barnardo's of Grafton Street, established in 1819, for your fur coat. Here, too, West's have for generations produced beautiful, expertly-designed and expensive items of jewellery.

There was a time when you could buy your hardware in Parke's of the Coombe, an old trading house which made many Dublin firms' trading tokens. A huge fire destroyed the premises in latter years and they never re-opened. Thomas Mason traded for many years in Palace Street, just beside the Castle, until a disastrous fire gutted his shop. Over the years, he had built up a large collection of photographic plates but these, too, were lost in the fire. His shop has now been replaced by the Millenium Park, with its three goddesses of wood, stone and metal. Close by, a plaque marks the birthplace of Barnardo, who founded the Children's Homes.

Thomas Read's of 4 Parliament Street, established in 1670, is one of the oldest cutlers in the world. They have a knife which has 576 different blades on it. They also have a Lilliputian pair of scissors, measuring a quarter-of-an-inch. Read's originally started business at the Blind Quay near Fishamble Street but later moved to Crane Lane which, incidentally, gets its name not from the bird but from the crane that unloaded goods at the quays opposite. They remained in Crane Lane until the Wide Streets Commissioners laid out Parliament Street. When the street was widened, Read's turned the shop around, the back of the shop and works becoming the front and the front becoming the back! They still retain a workshop in Crane Lane where knives, scissors and all kinds of implements are repaired and sharpened.

The interior of the shop is full of atmosphere, a real throwback to times gone by. Many of the display cases, drawers and counters are from the original shop. Read's also made swords and surgical instruments and, in the days when the surgeons from the College in Stephen's Green were breaking new ground in their profession, Read's got the job of making and designing the instruments from the surgeons' rough sketches.

COMMERCIAL LIFE

Carton was another old name. You could go to Carton Bros. of Halston Street for eggs, butter, cheese, poultry and game and to E. & D. Carton of Smithfield for corn, hay, potatoes, seed, grain etc. Dublin's cattle market was at one time held in Smithfield and this accounted for many of the old merchants still to be found in the Square. But these become fewer and fewer as the years go by.

The courtyard of Carton's has a real old-world feel about it. Even today, it is not unusual to find a horse-and-cart arriving to collect fodder and other supplies, even though C. Dodd and Sons, one of the main firms in this line of business, is gone. Jameson's Distillery, across the cobbled square, is no longer is use.

For many years, the area round Dame Street and College Green has been

The interior of Read's Cutlery shop, showing some of the original sword cases.

insurance land. The Sun Insurance Company, founded in 1710, claims to be the oldest in the world but the Commercial Union claims to go back to 1696. The fire brigade service was once run by the insurance companies but they only threw water and sand on the houses that were insured and many a merchant regretted the day he forgot to pay his premium. Before this the parish churches organised the pumps, buckets and ladders, each parish acting as its own fire-service. Today's Dublin Fire Brigade is a descendant of the service run by the insurance companies.

Yes, we had umbrella merchants and clock merchants but what about a gas merchant? 'You're a gas merchant' meant that you were terribly funny. The dentist was the first gas merchant. To stop you roaring with pain, he gave

A. G. WALLER,
Undertaker,
Carriage Proprietor, Furniture Removal Contractor, and Coal Merchant.

48, 49, 50 Denzille Street,
Merrion Square. and

41, 42 SANDWITH STREET, DUBLIN.

CARRIAGES OF EVERY DESCRIPTION FOR HIRE. WITH RUBBER TYRES, PER HOUR. MONTH. YEAR. etc.

Appointments First Class.   Moderate Terms.

Telephone 131.   Telegrams: "UNDERTAKER. DUBLIN."

A versatile businessman of 1917.

COMMERCIAL LIFE

you laughing gas so that you laughed instead and thus the dentist became known as the gas merchant among other names. I remember one time saying to someone: 'Yer man is a gas merchant.' 'No, he's not,' said my friend, 'he works in the Corporation.'

Markets, markets, markets. Here are a few names once familiar to Dubliners – The Camden, The Castle, Mason's, The Food, Potato and Fruit Markets. There was also the Leinster Market, pushed out of the way to make room for the Gas Company in D'Olier Street. The Bird Market in Dublin has a long history. It moved from time to time around the Liberties of Dublin. For years it stood in Bride Street at the rear of St Patrick's Cathedral, opposite Wood Street. Many a child went home from the Bird Market carrying a white paper bag thinking it contained a bird. 'Mister, Mister, give us a bird; give us a bird, Mister.' To get rid of the non-buying children, the dealers would stick their hand into a paper bag, twist the top of it and say: 'There now and don't open the bag until you get home.' On the complaining child's return to the market, the dealer would convince him it must have flown out of the bag. 'Go away out of that,' he would say. 'You lost the bloody one I gave you last week. Go down to the Cats' and Dogs' Home and get yourself a wow-wow.'

'Two shillings each the yellow canaries. How about a nice budgie? I'll have eagles next.' The Bird Market goes back hundreds of years and was always very popular with Dublin people. In the early days the birds were sold by sailors who came into Dublin on foreign ships. At one time the bird was carried home in your pocket or hands. Later still it was in brown or white paper bags or black sugar bags.

The glamour of the markets remains. In fact, Dublin is again becoming a city of markets. It's a far cry from the Daily to the Dandelion or from the Iveagh to the Liberty. Moore Street, Thomas Street, Henry Street, Francis

Street, Liffey Street at Christmas time, all have markets, big and small. Hector Grey no longer sells at the Ha'penny Bridge, though his son still owns the pitch. The Balloon Man, the tin whistles and 'the last of the long decorations' are still familiar to the real Dubliner.

You can buy a bronze bracelet, prints of Dublin, books by the dozen, a chamberpot, a hall table, an umbrella, shoes for every shape and size of foot, long-Johns or jockey briefs, hot pants, mini-skirts, maxi dresses and leather skirts, drawers, belts, bags and boots.

Any day of the week you will find the streets around the fruit and vegetable market off Capel Street blocked with orange boxes, crates of apples, bananas and forklift trucks. Nearby a man in huge rubber boots and a long apron is hosing down the floor of the Fish Market. Both markets are run by the Corporation and traders rent stalls to sell and auction their produce.

Nearby, in East Arran Street, old ladies rummage through huge piles of jackets, coats, frocks and shoes. This is the Daisy Market. It dates back a long way and some of the women have been selling here for fifty years.

Just off Moore Street the last tattered remains of the Anglesea Markets are now replaced by the modern ILAC shopping mall. Business is still going on, but the lot will soon come crumbling down when the Corporation presses ahead with its new plans for this area.

The cattle market between Prussia Street and the North Circular Road is now quiet. But it was not long ago that cattle were driven through these streets and small boys with big sticks beat the poor beasts on their way to the quays for export.

So get up on your bike and do a tour of Dublin markets and you are bound to come home with a bargain or two.

COMMERCIAL LIFE

A TRIP DOWN THE PORT

EVERY NOW AND THEN, A FEW MEN dressed in bright yellow oilskin coats and hats stand on O'Connell Bridge collecting funds for the Royal National Lifeboat Institution. You can put your donation into a boat-shaped box or into a pipeline running from the bridge to a lifeboat, gaily decorated with flags and bunting, in the River Liffey. These are the men that go down to the sea, risking their lives to save others in distress in heavy seas off the port of Dublin.

Look! They are moving off. Let's go with them and explore the port. We're moving now in the ripples of the gunboat, *Helga*, which travelled these waters in 1916 to shell Liberty Hall and Dublin city. On your right is Burgh Quay. The Scotch House pub once stood here but has been knocked down. Around the corner is Hawkins Street, named after a man who planned the Hawkins Wall to push back the river Liffey and reclaim the land at Burgh Quay. Next

A notice near Mountjoy Jail dating from the days when cattle were driven up these streets to and from the market between Prussia Street and North Circular Road.

ME JEWEL AND DARLIN' DUBLIN

From the Illustrated London News of 1873. This view shows the port, the Custom House, and Amiens Street Railway Station.

you will see the Corn Exchange and the Conciliation Hall used by the Young Irelanders and the Repeal Association. Then comes the *Irish Press* newspaper group building, where Padraig Pearse's mother started the printing presses to produce the first issue in 1931. The name '*Irish Press*' came from J. J. McGarrity's old newspaper in Philadelphia.

Liberty Hall, the home of Larkin, Connolly, Mallin and Partridge, soars skywards; it was originally the Northumberland Hotel. Liberty Hall was the first trade union headquarters in Dublin. The sign over the door read: 'We serve neither King nor Kaiser but Ireland.' The Irish Citizen Army, in their green and grey uniforms, together with their Chief of Staff, Michael Mallin, spent time practising foot and arms drill in Beresford Lane. Willie Oman,

COMMERCIAL LIFE

the bugler, has just sounded the fall-in. Pearse has arrived with the boys of *Scoil Éanna*, and that is James Connolly standing on the steps. Now we pass under two bridges, Butt Bridge spanning the Liffey and the Loop Line railway bridge above the busy thoroughfare. Isaac Butt, the Fenians' friend, took their brief in Green Street courthouse. He became a pauper, was locked in the debtor's prison without a friend and died in loneliness.

Dublin's glory, Dublin's pride and joy, James Gandon's Custom House is a beauty in stone, with its green dome, its clock, its long room, its steps and its gardens. Look back and have a clear view. Dubliners can't see it from the city side because their view is cut off by the Loop line which should never have been built here. The stone carvings were designed by Edward Smyth. There are fourteen beautiful keystones, one for Anna Livia, one for the Atlantic Ocean and twelve for the principal rivers in Ireland. It is the finest Custom House in the world. John Beresford laid the foundation stone and the building was opened in 1791. The architect, James Gandon, born in England, was the grandson of a Huguenot who fled from France on the Revocation of the Edict of Nantes. During the Black-and-Tan days, the Dublin IRA burned the Custom House which contained huge numbers of records of the British Administration system. It has been said that this action was one of the factors which led to the truce of July 1921.

This port dates back to the Bronze Age when Dubliners sailed from here to cross the seven seas. Our exports were gold and copper from the Wicklow mines. Trade and shipping became so heavy over the years that the larger boats could only come as far as the Pool of Clontarf and others had to land at Dalkey and Dun Laoghaire (Kingstown). Improvements were made in the 13th century but still the port couldn't cope with all the ships. As each decade went by more improvements were carried out and, in 1649, Oliver Cromwell

Dublin's glory – James Gandon's Custom House viewed from the other side of the Liffey.

landed his ships and 13,000 soldiers at Ringsend.

The merchants of Dublin still pressed the Dublin Corporation for more developments, including clearing the port of ballast dumped by incoming ships. The Corporation wouldn't spend the few shillings so the merchants petitioned Queen Anne and bribed her husband with a hundred yards of best Holland Duck sail-cloth. Yer man took the bribe. The Queen passed the Act and the Dublin Corporation had to set up a special committee to look after the port and ballast.

The year 1707 was the start of a great era for the port with plans being made for the new South Wall and later the North Wall. The Bull Wall, designed by the port's own engineer, George Halpin, was added in 1820. Captain Bligh (of *The Bounty*) paid a visit to advise on development matters and also the Poolbeg Lighthouse. The idea of the Bull Wall was to quicken the speed of the ebbing tide, free the bay of obstacles and give greater force to the waters into the port. The Bull Wall gave us the Bull Island, where today we have one of the world's finest and most important wildlife breeding grounds. Here is

COMMERCIAL LIFE

a bird sanctuary in a capital city with the greatest collection in numbers and types of wild fowl. For students who are studying nature and wildlife, it is a Paradise.

The 100-ton crane which was brought into the port nearly ninety years ago has recently been dismantled, but you can still see Misery Hill where the old lepers lived and where the City Sheriff had his hanging-ground. The road beyond leads to Raytown (Ringsend) and the old Pidgeon House, named after John Pidgeon, who was caretaker of tools and equipment at the building of the South Wall. The Pidgeon House later became a musical tavern, a military post and now it is an electricity generating station.

There was a time around 1936 when you could take a trip around the port and bay of Dublin in the *Royal Iris* for half-a-crown.

*Meetinghouse Lane. On the left is the small door which
leads to the Chapter House of Mary's Abbey.*

CHAPTER 5

HIDDEN PLACES

AROUND ST MARY'S ABBEY

NOW IT WAS LIKE THIS. On a warm September afternoon, in the 11th century, Clunlif and his wife Dervogil were sitting outside their house and vast lands on the northern banks of the river Liffey. Clunlif Gill Moholomoc was one of the high-ranking chiefs of Dublin and was the owner of a fair bit of property inside the walls of Dublin City. Clunlif was stone-blind, as was his closest kinsman, Malachi. I suppose this was the reason he chose to live beyond the walls and waters of Dublin.

Well, himself and the wife were enjoying the sunshine and at the same time giving alms to the poor who were always welcome. Suddenly, Clunlif, who was sitting on the log of a tree, got the sweet smell of the apple blossom. He put his hand along the tree log, felt an apple, plucked it and bit hard into its juicy centre. His eyes opened and for the first time in many years he could see the Danish Fort, the Liffey waters, his kinsmen, his wife and his lands. He then saw two more apples on the log. He called his wife and Malachi. They both ate of the fruit and Malachi's sight was restored. The miracle would not be forgotten, for Clunlif was a holy, generous man. Soon the trio, Clunlif, Dervogil and Malachi, decided to erect an Abbey which they would dedicate to Mary, the mother of God. The Abbey was handed over to the followers of St Benedict, known as The Black Monks.

In 1139, the Benedictines adopted the Cistercian rule and got the full approval and blessing of Pope Eugenius III. The Abbey of St Mary claimed all the lands north of the Liffey from their Abbey House, which stood near Ormond Quay, to the lands of Clunlif (Clonliffe) at Drumcondra, beside the Tolka river. In the other direction, they claimed the fields of Oxmantown to Salock Woods at the Phoenix Park swinging gates. The Abbot and his monks became very rich and influential. They had their own fleet of vessels and their own herring-sheds and claimed not only taxes on the fish from the Liffey but on everything that sank or was shipwrecked on the Liffey bed.

They had the best of both worlds and got a Liberty from King Henry II and another Liberty from the Pope in Rome. Henry's charter confirmed all their claims to land and property within and without the walls of Dublin City. King John, who followed Henry in the 13th century, gave several charters to the Abbey and placed the monks under his direct care. They were also under the direct care of Rome. The wealth and influence of the Abbey increased and the Abbot sat in Parliament as a spiritual Lord with a temporal eye. The Abbot soon adopted the same customs as the Abbot of the Liberty of St Thomas Court and Donore. He had his Abbey church, his palace, his dungeons and his gallows and sat at times as a Lord Chief Justice.

Down the years some of the Abbots considered themselves more powerful than the English King or the Roman Pope. In 1214, when the Prior and Canons of Christ Church Cathedral tried to cut in on the Abbot's treasure, they were opposed with words and swords. Christ Church backed down but a decree of excommunication was issued against the Abbot and monks of St Mary's Abbey. One year later, Felix O'Ruadan, Archbishop of Tuam, came to St Mary's Abbey and stated that he had resigned and wished to spend the rest of his days as a simple monk. The graves of Felix, Clunlif, Dervogil and Malachi and the monks and Abbots who died before the suppression lie under the roadway of Capel Street and Mary's Abbey.

The only remaining relics today are the lands of Clonliffe (Holy Cross College) and the Chapter House in Meetinghouse Lane, off Mary's Abbey. St Mary's is under the care of the Board of Works and is now open to the public. It is well worth a visit to see the Council Chamber where in 1534 Silken Thomas threw down the Sword of State and went into rebellion against the English Crown. Silken Thomas's father, the Earl of Kildare and Lord Deputy of Ireland, had been summoned to London and a rumour reached Ireland that he had been murdered in the Tower of London.

Silken Thomas, so called because of his fancy clothes, marched into the Council Chamber and, instead of taking his father's place at the head of the table, began to curse the King of England. The wise Lords tried to quieten

Newgate Jail, demolished long ago, which adjoined Green Street Courthouse.

him. 'Keep calm,' they said. 'Wait for more news. Send a messenger. Wait, don't rush.' Silken Thomas was about to sit down when one of his followers plucked the strings of a Geraldine war-harp with the Earl's battle tune. The music boiled the blood of Silken Thomas and down went the sword. 'To hell with the King,' he said, and stormed from the Chamber to head an attack on the Castle and Dublin city. The rebellion failed. Silken Thomas was invited to London for peace talks. As soon as he and his five uncles arrived, they were put in chains and later hanged at Tyburn Cross.

The statue of Our Lady of Dublin in Whitefriars Street Church (Aungier Street) is another relic of St Mary's Abbey. This statue, carved in wood, has a strange history. For several hundred years it was used as a pigs' water trough in East Arran Street. Then, in 1824, Rev. John Spratt, prior of the Carmelite Order, discovered and purchased it in a second-hand junk shop in Capel Street. East Arran Street was originally Boot Lane, with its several alleys and rows of unusual names – Manypenny Yard, Brush Row, Lucky Hall and Petticoat Lane, all leading to Green Street court-house, the 'new' Newgate Jail, George's Hill and Cuckoo Lane.

Today a handball alley, a children's playground, a few seats for old men and women and a memorial statue mark the site of the jail which was demolished in 1893. It was here that Lord Edward Fitzgerald died in his prison cell and the Sheares brothers, John and Henry, stood side-by-side waiting on the hangman's axe outside the Newgate door.

Green Street court-house, which is still in use today, has been the place of trial for Republicans and separatists since 1796. The first Belfast Republican to enter its door was John Robb, printer of *The Northern Star*, the official organ of The United Irishmen's Society. In September 1796, Robb, Samuel Neilson (the editor) and Thomas Russell arrived. They had been arrested on a sedition charge, taken from their homes in Belfast and driven non-stop by horse cart, day and night, to Newgate Jail.

In 1970, a descendant of John Robb, bearing the same name, and noted as one of the North's most respected moderates, showed me and others in The Tailors' Hall, Back Lane, a number of letters and keepsakes dating back to 1796. Under the court-house are the same cells used by Emmet, his men and the men of 1798. John Mitchel and the Young Irelanders, Rossa and the Fenians, and the Irish National Invincibles – Brady, Curley, Kelly, Caffrey, Fagan, and 'Skin the Goat' – also spent time here.

In the year 1815, the last public whipping took place from the gates of Green Street court-house to City Hall (Royal Exchange) on Cork Hill. The victim was William Horish, 'the master sweep', who lived in Dame Court. This was by no means the first whipping that William Horish had received. In July 1803, he was arrested on the word of an informer named Carroll and taken to Tyrone House. This large stone building in Marlborough Street, known as Beresford's Riding House Establishment, was used as a torture and flogging house in 1798 and 1803. It appears that Major Sirr failed to break Horish's spirit and continued to harass and torture him on trumped-up charges, even twelve years after Emmet's Rising.

Before we leave this haunted centre of Dublin, spare a thought for the scores who went to their deaths and left their last letters, written to wives, children, fathers, mothers and other relations, in the hands of Major Sirr. He never delivered the letters but kept them in his own private papers. They are now in the archives of Trinity College.

Beyond Green Street lies 'George's Hill', the convent school of Teresa Mullally, Nano Nagle and the Presentation Sisters. Teresa was born in Pill Lane (Chancery Street) in 1728. Her ambition in life was to found a school and teach children. Despite Castle spies and priest-hunters, she rented, at her own expense, a house in Mary's Lane and, from a small class of twelve children, she built up several other classes until she decided she needed a larger building to cater for her pupils. In 1787 she moved her school to the old glassworks on George's Hill. A friendship with a girl named Nano Nagle led to the introduction of the Presentation Nuns to George's Hill.

After the suppression of St Mary's Abbey, the lands became the property of King Henry VIII, who gave them to Henry Moore, Earl of Drogheda. Henry Street, Moore Street, Earl Street and even O'Connell Street, formerly Drogheda Street, were named after this Henry Moore. The next owner was a man named John Piphoe, a son of Adam Piphoe of Clontarf Castle. When Piphoe died, the lands were claimed by his widow. However, Dublin Castle had other ideas and tried to take the land from her. After enquiries, it was found that the old lady was ninety-eight years old and very frail. 'Ah, leave it with her,' they said. 'Sure she will be dead in a few weeks.' Dead, how are you! She lived another twenty years and saw many of the Castle grabbers under the clay before she finally died in 1669 at the age of 118 years. Her grave is in the vaults of St Michan's Church.

Jervis Street gets its name from the next owner of the lands of St Mary's Abbey. Sir Humphrey Jervis, Lord Mayor of Dublin, built a bridge across the Liffey facing Dublin Castle and also laid out Capel Street and the adjoining streets. He gave the first choice in naming them to the Viceroy who in 1678 was Arthur Capel, Earl of Essex. So we have Capel Street, Essex Street, Essex Quay and Essex Bridge. Jervis Street, named after himself, once enjoyed the distinction of having Dublin's first and oldest hospital built on it. The old Charitable Infirmary, later called Jervis Street Hospital, dates from 1718. It no longer operates as a hospital and there are plans to turn it into another

Old St Mary's Church (no longer in use as a church) viewed from Wolfe Tone Street. Sean O'Casey was baptised here.

shopping mall. One of the wards in the old hospital faced the street where Wolfe Tone was born in June 1763. Formerly Stafford Street, it is now named after the patriot. Another ward overlooked St Mary's Church and graveyard.

This church, dating back to 1691, is steeped in history and was one of the first churches in Dublin to display on a notice-board its historic traditions and connections with Dublin and Ireland's history. It was here that Tone and Sean O'Casey were baptised. The park beside the church is well laid out and contains a memorial stone to Wolfe Tone.

The next time you are coming down Capel Street, think of Number 27 (the houses have since been re-numbered) and try to imagine poor King James II making coins from tin cans, pots and pans, cannon gun and cannon balls. Yes, this was James's mint. But after the Battle of the Boyne, King Billy came down Capel Street and kicked the tin cans all around St Mary's Abbey. Did you ever play 'Kick the Can' when you were a child? All you want is a tin can and a good pair of hobnail boots with iron tips on the toes and heels.

James minted nearly a million pounds between 18 June 1689, and 15 June 1690. Money valued by James at £21,886 was worth only £642 in real terms. Ah, it's a pity you're dead, James! You died too soon. Sure in 1972 I saw an advert in *Irish Numismatics*, the coin magazine, offering for sale 'a James II Gunmoney Crown struck in gold' for £5000.

Well, thank you, Sir Humphrey Jervis. You didn't do a bad job. Fair play to ya. Your Jervis Street has another proud distinction. It provided a birthplace for Dublin's greatest historian, Sir John T. Gilbert, author of three volumes on the history of the old city and south-side of Dublin. His attention to detail in the *Calendar of Ancient Records of Dublin* is monumental. Volume after volume he produced and recorded the White Book, the Blue Book, the Chain Book and the city clock which the Corpo was going to give to Oxmantown because the fellows in Thomas Street would not wind it every day. They say Gilbert never wrote a word about the northside or the place of his birth. Sometimes we are inclined to forget his *Chartularies of St Mary's Abbey*.

If you can find the time, take a trip down the steps to the stone Chapter House. When you step onto the stone floor about eight feet down, you are at the original street level of Dublin town eight hundred years ago. If ever the houses and buildings around this area are knocked down, the National Museum should move in, for under the ground is the buried treasure of Dublin's history and its great abbey.

THE FIVE LAMPS

THE FIVE LAMPS STAND ON A CONCRETE ISLAND at the junction of five roads. Let's make five short tours, all within five minutes from the five lamps.

HIDDEN PLACES

The Five Lamps with Aldborough House behind. Five streets meet here – Amiens Street, North Strand Road, Portland Row, Seville Place and Killarney Street.

1. Across the road is Aldborough House with memories of Edward Stratford, Viscount Amiens, Earl of Aldborough. He had the house built in 1796 and it cost £40,000. It was another Georgian beauty and the last of the great town-houses of the period but the wife didn't like it. She said it was too damp and too near Mud Island. So back she went to Stratford-on-Avon. However, they came back again to build the town of Stratford-on-Slaney in County Wicklow. Edward even had a theatre in Aldborough House but it was a bit of a flop.

The house was then rented by Von-Feinagle for his Feinaglian School. He named the school 'Luxembourg College' and had a system of education on the exercise of the memory. There were no blackboards, chalk or writing books, just a system for memorising every subject and keeping it at the finger-tips. He turned 'scholars' out the gate in their dozens. He died in 1819 and the house became vacant for a few years. The Red-Coat soldiers used it as a temporary barracks and, in 1843, when Dan O'Connell organised his Clontarf meeting, the barracks was filled with 3,000 troops. Dan called off the meeting and sent special messengers to notify several people in person. The messengers conveyed the sad news to the people who had marched from Wexford and they just hung about in groups under the eyes of the Red-Coats beside the Five Lamps.

2. Running between Summerhill and Amiens Street is Buckingham Street. No, it's not called after the Palace but after the Viceroy, the Marquess of Buckingham. Did you know that one of the Buckinghams gave us the first miniskirt? Well, it happened like this. The King of England always washed his hands after a day's hunting and Buckingham's job was to hold the bucket of water. This day, as he was holding the bucket, didn't Cardinal Wolsey come in before the King; 'Oh, good,' he said and dipped his dirty maulers into the bucket of water. Buckingham was furious, so he threw the bucket, water and all, over Wolsey. 'I'll get you, Buckingham,' he said. 'Tomorrow, in the House of Lords, I'll tread on the tail of your coat.' The next day, Buckingham appeared wearing only a leather jerkin (mini-skirt size!). 'You won't get a chance to tread on my coat-tails,' he said to the King. 'This is the length of my coat from now on.'

Number 36 Buckingham Street was the home of John O'Donovan, the father of a family of Fenians. One of his sons, also named John, manufactured rifles and bullets in this house. Rossa, Stephens, Thomas Clarke and Luby held Council meetings in the front parlour. Across the road, where the pawn office used to stand, was the local Royal Irish Constabulary barracks. Little did the 'polis' know that a Fenian headquarters was right opposite their hall door. John O'Donovan was a great scholar and translated many Gaelic manuscripts, including the works of the Four Masters in 1864. Because of his great learning, he had many academic friends, including the Provost and several Fellows of Trinity College. The ancient *Annals of the Kingdom of Ireland* and the *Martyrology of Donegal*, a calendar of the saints of Ireland, written by the Four Masters in 1630, lay in dust for 234 years until they were transcribed by O'Curry and translated by John O'Donovan in Buckingham Street, Dublin.

At the top of the hill, turn to the right and look into Ballybough, 'the town of the poor,' noted today for racing pigeons and luxury pigeon lofts. Go around to the right again and into Portland Row and down the hill back to the Five Lamps.

3. Do you see the railway bridge? Well, if you don't, walk once around the Five Lamps and you're sure to spot it. What did you say? You saw two. Well, I need only one for my story or the Five Lamps, Five Tours, Five Minutes will lose its appeal. During the last war, 555 State Express cigarettes were a Godsend to smokeless Dublin. They also manufactured State Express 333 and the little shop at the corner had buckets of them.

Look down Seville Place. Better still, walk down to the bridge and notice St Laurence O'Toole's Church standing in the distance. The Pagan O'Leary helped build that one too and Joe Clarke went to school beside it. The master used to mark his boots with white chalk when he missed his lessons. But even then Joe was a rebel. He used to rub out the chalk marks and the master could never remember whether he had marked them or not. Every Monday morning, our laundry van passed down Seville Place and I always had a good look at the church and the iron gate at the end of Guild Street. The gate seemed to draw me and I often wondered what it was about it that compelled me to look at it. Fourteen years later, I was the manager of a coal-yard behind that iron gate in Guild Street. Across the road from it were Synott's and Kilbride's shop and, in Black-and-Tan days, the iron gate led into an IRA arms dump.

Guild Street leads to Dublin dockland with Spencer Dock on the waterfront. This was another world, another city with talk of fillers, breasters, casuals and button men, screening, tapping out, lower your gib, singer-outs and hooker-ons. At one time it was no work in the rain, no money to spare, just 'under the hammer' and the £5 Christmas 'kick' paid back by the week, Beero hour, the Jade, the Myrtle, or Polish coal which was called continental for fear of religious reaction. I know you're thinking this is a hairy five minutes' walk from the Five Lamps, so I'd better stop or next I'll have you in the ferry crossing the river to the great South Wall. The bridge at Seville Place was where Joe Poole shot the informer. Joe was an Invincible and was later hanged in Richmond Jail. The story of Pat O'Donnell and James Carey is well-known but little is known today of Joseph Poole, who shot the first informer under the ridge down the street from the Five Lamps.

4. Now don't tell me it's more than five minutes' walk to Gloucester Street. Well, even if its ten, it's worth going there to see the Street, the Diamond, the Place and Kane's Court. This is really Kane country. The Duke of Gloucester was only the son of a King, but Robert Kane was the son of a Dublin scientist. He was born in Gloucester Street on 24 September, 1809. At an early age, he showed great interest in his father's work, chemistry. The father taught the son well and young Robert entered the Meath Hospital as a medical student. Before he was twenty-one, he was Professor of Chemistry in the Apothecaries Hall, a position he held for fourteen years. He published several books and founded the *Dublin Journal of Medical Science*. Kane's works, his life, his teaching and industrial ideas would fill many volumes.

He loved Dublin and Ireland and was in a sense the first Sinn Féiner (Ourselves Alone). He made proposals for water power at Shannon and also peat power. He produced plans for the use of glass, sand and gypsum and preached the urgent need for agricultural education. If the authorities had listened to Kane and acted as he advised, the Famine might never have happened. Go into the National Library and get the books of Robert Kane and discover the mind of this great man who was born in Dublin down the street from the Five Lamps.

A turn off the street where Kane was born brings you into Cumberland Street. Here was the birthplace of Sir Charles Cameron, the greatest Medical Health Officer that Dublin City ever had, a man who saved the lives of thousands of Dubliners and who rid Dublin of its fever epidemics. He was head of the Freemason Order, yet spent his life working for the poor of Dublin who were 95 percent Catholic. He was a legend in his lifetime and I wonder what he would say today if he could see the poor of Dublin buying second-hand clothes from the gutters in the street where he was born.

5. The bridge at The Royal Canal at North Strand Road is the spot where Matt Talbot decided to give up the drink and lead his holy life. The bridge is named Newcomen after a director of The Royal Canal. Beyond the bridge lies Bessborough Avenue, which brings to mind Dublin's association with two ladies and blue stockings – Lady Eleanor Butler of Kilkenny Castle and her friend, Sarah Ponsonby, who came from the family of the Earls of Bessborough. The girls ran away together and settled down in a house in the vale of Llangollen. For over seventy years they were known as the Ladies of Llangollen and were often visited by many Earls and Lords of Ireland and England. They lived contented lives among their books and gardens and knitted blue stockings. They were both 90 years of age when they died, Lady Butler in 1829 and Miss Ponsonby in 1831. I visited their home, which today is a tourist attraction. It is in a beautiful vale, miles from anywhere, and I could almost see them

sitting in their garden, drinking tea which had just been served by their Irish maid, Mary Carroll. It's a far cry from Llangollen, Wales, to the North Strand, Dublin, but then many names in Dublin have a cry to the end of the earth.

The Five Lamps were erected as a memorial to General Henry Hall, a native of Galway who served in the Indian Army, so they have links with the Punjab, Aliwal, and other Indian battles where Irishmen fell in their thousands. Ninety percent of the British Indian Army were recruited during the famine days when the choice for many was to starve to death or to see glory, travel the world, have Indian servants and a horse, a sword, a smart uniform, full rations and beer daily. Pay was seven shillings a week, which was worth a fortune in India.

THE ROYAL CIRCUS

I'M SITTING IN THE MIDDLE OF The Royal Circus as I write these words but it's not exactly the type of private mansion Luke Gardiner had in mind as part of his grand design. The 1798 rebellion changed many things. It also killed Luke Gardiner at the battle of New Ross and deprived Dublin of its Royal Circus.

Mountjoy Jail was built as part of the Famine relief work. Its door was opened for guests in 1860 and it's still in business today. I have examined in detail for several hours its structure, its wall-thickness, the strength of its grille-type iron-barred windows and, you can take my word on it, it's a very solid structure, good for at least another hundred years. The builders of Mountjoy Jail did a bloody fine job for a few bowls of soup. I would hate to think what they would have built if they had been paid wages.

The reason the jail was built was because the people of Botany Bay complained to the King of England about all the convicts being dumped outside their hall doors. O'Donovan Rossa, manager of *The Irish People*, the Fenian newspaper, spent Christmas of 1865 inside Mountjoy Jail. Every day I walk in Rossa's footsteps around the exercise yard or look out into the wood yard where Thomas Ashe chopped wood for the jail boilers. The place is haunted with memories. (I nearly spent Christmas of 1973 here, but like many others was whisked away to Portlaoise prison following a surprise helicopter escape.) I cannot help wondering how many more editors of *An Phoblacht* will spend time here.

Fifteen paces from my cell leads to the hang-house door. There are times when I can almost see Kevin Barry, head erect, walking past me to meet his God. The story of the jail would fill many books and perhaps some day a pen will scribe words into a volume named 'Mountjoy Jail Journal'.

Luke Gardiner, Lord Mountjoy, was the largest land-owner on the north side of Dublin City. He was the man whose family built Sackville Street, Mountjoy Square and the other North Dublin Georgian avenues and he him-

The sad face of Mountjoy Square in recent times. No. 50, centre, has since been demolished, despite efforts by the Irish Georgian Society to save it.

self had plans to build a Royal Circus where the Mater Hospital and Mountjoy Jail stand today. The Royal Circus was to consist of several splendid private Georgian mansions, miniatures of Castletown House, Celbridge, with twelve grand avenues leading into the circus. It was to be a question of the richer you are, the nearer you live to The Royal Circus. Those in the Circus itself were to have been the elite of the elite.

The plans were drawn up and the first avenue, Eccles Street, was actually laid out on the site of the gardens of Mount Eccles House, the residence of Sir John Eccles, Lord Mayor of Dublin in 1710. Synott Place, Cowley Place and Elizabeth Street were decided on as three other avenues. However, the 1798 Rebellion was erupting and Luke Gardiner cast aside his Royal Circus plans and rode to Wexford at the head of the Dublin Militia. That was the last time Luke saw Dublin. He was killed in action and, with his death, work on the Royal Circus stopped and Luke's plans were never completed.

Across Eccles Street from the Mater Hospital (1861), stands a Celtic Cross, a monument to the Four Masters. Why it was erected here is a mystery. The Franciscans asked for it to be erected beside their friary on Merchants' Quay but their wishes were ignored. The monument is almost hidden behind railings at the corner of Eccles Street and Berkeley Road. The inscription is in Irish, English and Latin.

The *Annals of the Kingdom of Ireland* are commonly known as the 'Annals of the Four Masters'. The contents took more than ten years to gather. Moore, in his *History of Ireland*, says: 'The precision with which the Irish Annalists have recorded month, day, hour of an eclipse of the sun in the year 664 affords an instance of the exceeding accuracy with which they observed and noted passing events.' Dublin is mentioned more than 250 times in the Annals, which were completed in 1637. Some of the recording was carried out in Dublin.

HIDDEN PLACES

Dublin had neglected the Four Masters until Sir Robert William Wilde suggested in *The Nation* newspaper of November 1871 that a memorial be erected. He was dead before the task was completed in 1876. We can be very certain that he never intended his dream to be hidden in a spot where it is unnoticed by the thousands who visit the Mater Hospital.

If you walk slowly down Eccles Street, you might meet Joyce's Leopold Bloom who lived in Number 7 or Brendan Behan's 'Hostage' being taken into a house in Nelson Street. If you see the Sheriff on his horse outside Number 64 Eccles Street, he is waiting to take Isaac Butt, the Home Rule leader, to the Debtors' prison. Francis Johnston, the architect of St George's Church, lived in the same house years before.

Francis Johnston was born in Armagh in 1760 and came to Dublin when he was a teenager. He was taught by Thomas Cooley, the man who designed the Royal Exchange, now the City Hall. Johnston designed many other fine buildings, including the G.P.O. in O'Connell Street (1814). His masterpiece is St George's Church in Hardwicke Street, which dates from 1802 and cost almost £90,000 to build. It stands 200 feet high with a five-storey clock tower and spire over its roof, which can be seen all over Dublin. St George's is no longer in use as a church and the spire is in need of repair. A great pity! The Iron Duke, Sir Arthur Wellesley, K.B., Duke of Wellington, married Catherine Sarah Dorothea Pakenham in St George's on 10 April, 1806.

In 1823, Francis Johnston took the eight bells, which he used to chime regularly to the annoyance of his neighbours, from his back garden and presented them to St George's Church. He was just in time because the first peal of the muffled bells in St George's was for his own funeral.

Beside the church in Temple Street is the Children's Hospital and Number 14 in the same street was the home of Charles Stewart Parnell and also the hiding place of many Fenians on the run. The street down the hill leads to the Old, or the Little, St George's Church, which dates back to the beginning of the 18th century. This is all Luke Gardiner, Lord Mountjoy land. It was Luke who gave the site for St George's Church. Its cemetery is off the Whitworth Road, beside Drumcondra Hospital.

If you haven't seen St George's you have missed a noble sight. Its spire can view the Royal Way or the old mailcoach road to Drumcondra, where you find the nicest Dublin accent and a good drop to drink in the old Cat and Cage tavern. The spire is a comforting sight, a beautiful sight, from the barred windows of Mountjoy Jail.

Maybe Luke got his Royal Circus after all. The Jail has a circle and four grand avenues – A Wing, B Wing, C Wing and D Wing – and I don't think there is a more private residence in Dublin. It is burglar-proof from outside and inside and, if anyone calls to visit you, you can always send word to the gate to say you're always at home.

PHOENIX PARK

'MISTER! MISTER! DO YOU WANT any weight, Mister?' A chorus of voices from dozens of children standing at the Park gates, offering themselves to the lorry drivers. A nod of the head and soon a dozen or more were hiding under the tarpaulin or empty sacks and wooden creels. As soon as the tare weight was taken, the lorry left the weighbridge and emptied its human cargo, paid their wages (two pence a child) and continued on to the fuel depot in the Phoenix Park. War years with ration books, a half-ounce of tea and the Phoenix Park turned into a turf-yard. Will the Park ever be the same again? Gone, too, are the days of Stanley Woods and the motor-bike racing and the Bluebird racing-car driven by a Prince. The Gough Monument never looked the same without the sandbags all around it. We never knew whether the sandbags were to protect the racing drivers or General Gough sitting up on his horse. In later years, Gough lost his sword, then his head, and then he suddenly disappeared – horse, steps and all!

If you want to amuse children and at the same time have a bit of peace, take them up to the 'Monie Mount', the children's favourite name for the Wellington Monument in the Phoenix Park. It was raised in honour of the Duke of Wellington, the man who helped to defeat Napoleon and who was born in 24 Upper Merrion Street, Dublin. Yet he claimed he was a Londoner. 'But, Arthur,' his friends said, 'you were born in Dublin, you're a Dubliner'. The only answer he ever gave was: 'If I was born in a stable, it wouldn't mean I'm a bloody horse.' The original design for the monument was not completed because of lack of funds. What you can see today cost over £21,000, an expensive piece of playground equipment for the children of Dublin.

The Phoenix Park is really a child's paradise with the dog pond, the herd of deer, the horsemen riding, the Phoenix Pillar and the polo grounds. You can enjoy the flower gardens or feed the ducks or spend a few hours in the Zoological Gardens. Don't miss a ride on the horse-train and be sure to watch seals diving for their meals. Visit the Fifteen Acres to watch the various sports and listen to music in Donnelly's Hollow. For the courting couples, it's the Furry Glen; for the old folk it's a seat in the shade of an elm tree, where Davis, Dillon and Duffy founded *The Nation* newspaper in the year 1842. A short distance up the main road, in view of the Viceregal Lodge, Cavendish and Burke fell on 6 May, 1882. For that deed five men – Joe Brady, Tim Kelly, Dan Curley, Thomas Caffrey and Michael Fagan – went to the scaffold. If you look up the road, you might see a cab driven by James FitzHarris ('Skin the Goat') on his way to Green Street courthouse and sixteen years in prison in

Portlaoise Jail, choosing that in place of becoming an informer and accepting gold and a pardon.

These are ancient lands, robbed by Strongbow, worked by the monks of Kilmainham Priory, given to the King by John Rawson and rented to Sir Edward Fisher. Fisher built his residence on St Thomas's Hill, later exchanging it for land in Cornwall, and the King again became the Lord and Master. Fisher's house became the home of many Viceroys, including Oliver Cromwell's brother, Henry. One hundred years later, in 1740, the house was pulled down and a Magazine Fort erected. The Viceroys moved to the King's house which was built in a hollow beside the church in Chapelizod. This house was standing up to some twenty-five years ago. As a boy, I delivered laundry-baskets to a family named Dixon who lived in it. Even at thirteen years of age, I was aware that it was an important house. It had long Queen Anne-type windows, a square doorway which opened into a large hall and was beautifully furnished. I remember studying the statues of little boys and girls outside the door and in the gardens.

The house and grounds still stand in my memory. It was always the first stop every Wednesday morning on our delivery route to Leixlip Castle and the Bird's Nest Orphanage in Castletown House, Celbridge. We always delivered two baskets, one marked 'Lord and Lady Carew', the other marked 'Bird's Nest, Castletown'. That was in 1940 and I was paid two shillings and five pence a day to tour Dublin and its neighbourhood, visiting many historic places, houses and castles. The Viceroys later moved from the King's house to the residence in the Phoenix Park. Go up today, explore and discover the finest park in the world, let the children run around, open up your picnic basket, relax and enjoy the air. You'll find it hard to believe that you are only a few minutes' drive from the hustle and bustle of the city streets.

HIDDEN PLACES

THE KING'S COWBOY

'LIBERTIES? LIBERTIES BE DAMNED! We'll get Napper Tandy and he'll soon put a stop to that fellow, John de Blaquiere. The cheek of him, anyway, trying to make a Liberty out of the people's Phoenix Park.' 'Ah, but he doesn't want it all, only thirty-five acres for his cows and bulls!' 'He won't even get a paddle in the dog pond when we're finished with him. There is only one thing to do,' said Napper Tandy. 'We'll take him to court. I'll go now and arrange for Barry Yelverton to take our brief.'

James Napper Tandy and the people
versus
Sir John Blacquiere

Blacquiere was Chief Secretary in Ireland and in 1774 he took the post of Bailiff of the Phoenix Park, which at the time entitled him to £9 a year and a small lodge. Shortly after this he decided, without permission, to fence off over 30 acres of the park near his residence. Blacquiere had no cause for concern. The three judges were his best friends and the jurymen were all picked for the occasion.

Not only did he win his Liberty and his land but he was awarded £8,000 out of the taxpayers' pocket to build a new residence, now the US Ambassador's residence. He later sold the lease for £7,000, even though the house was supposed to belong to the Castle.

The case was held in Green Street courthouse and the three judges ruled that 'it was only by leave of the King the citizens had liberty to recreate themselves under restrictions'. So Blacquiere's Liberty under the Crown also gave the Crown the absolute ownership of the Phoenix Park. And now that his decision had been approved of by the courts, Blacquiere organised a salary increase of £500 per annum as payment for his side-line task as Bailiff of the Phoenix Park, besides securing unlimited grazing for his cattle.

He continued to prosper and left his name on one of our bridges – Blacquiere Bridge in Phibsborough. But this section of the Royal Canal is now gone and we have a park in its place, so one one really sees the bridge. It is there beside the State Cinema which was once called the Blacquiere picture-house. So, in the words of the ballad-makers, in the year 1775 Blacquiere's Liberty –

Debarred the roads near our abodes
No car, nor coach shall pass,
Our cows alone (the soil's our own)
Shall eat the Royal Grass.

OLD KILMAINHAM

SURE YOU COULD WRITE A BOOK about it, and where will I start? A visit to the jail? The Royal Hospital? Bully's Acre? St John's Well? Major Sirr's Stag House? The Robber's Den? Nasan Browne's Inn? Or Gipsy Rose Lee's caravan home? In the sixth century, Saint Maigned built his church here and gave the district its name: *Cill Maigned*, the church of Maigned. The name became corrupted into Kilmainham. In 1014, on the way to Clontarf, Brian Boru rested his troops in the fields of Kilmainham. His son, Murrough, said: 'If I fall in battle, take my body back here and bury me on the hilltop.' Murrough fell and his grave lies today in Bully's Acre, a few yards from the graves of Emmet and the other heroes of the 1803 Rising.

Emmet's body was buried in Bully's Acre, though the records state that it was taken up a week later and given to the Rev. Mr Gamble of St Michan's Church. However, the body is not to be found in St Michan's vaults or churchyard. It is odd that Mr Gamble should wait a week to claim the body, because he stood beside Emmet in his last moments. The time and place to claim the body would have been the day and hour after Emmet's death. Why, then, would he have gone to so much trouble to allow the body to be taken back to Kilmainham Jail and then be buried in Bully's Acre before being brought back a week later to St Michan's? Bully's Acre is the only graveyard that was never searched for Emmet's body. It was to prevent people from visiting the grave that they were told it had been taken from Bully's Acre. A false entry could have been made in the records to prove this point. Denis Lamert-Redmond's last request was to be buried beside Robert Emmet. He was hanged on Wood Quay, yet his body was taken to Bully's Acre for burial. Let us search the Bully's Acre ground. Who knows? – the grave of Emmet might be lying in the shadows of Murrough's Cross.

The lands of Kilmainham, from the Royal Hospital gate across to the Hole in the Wall in the Phoenix Park and out to the home of Isolde, Princess of Dublin, in Chapelizod, were given by Strongbow to a Priory of St John the Baptist, which was founded in the year 1174. The Order of the Hospital of St John of Jerusalem, the fighting soldier-monks, continued in residence until they were suppressed in the 16th century.

The Duke of Ormonde became Viceroy in 1677 and between himself and King Charles II a decision was made to erect a soldier's hospital, similar to that in Chelsea, in the priory grounds. William Robinson was the architect chosen and Ormonde laid the foundation-stone of the Royal Hospital on 29 April 1680. In 1922, the last soldier-pensioners were transferred from here to Chelsea. During the late 1930s, the building was always referred to as the 'Old Men's Home'. Later it became the property of the Commissioner of Police.

The building still stands today as the Museum of Modern Art, and is used

Kilmainham Jail, Dublin. To the right is the court house, which is still in use.

for various State and other functions. It is open to the public and there is a quaint restaurant in what used to be the vaults. It also houses a Museum of Modern Art.

The Royal Hospital is a place worthy of a visit, with one of the finest clock-towers to be seen in Ireland. If the gates are locked, take a walk down John's Road and you will see the building and Bully's Acre graveyard from the roadway.

British soldiers killed during the 1916 Rising were buried in Bully's Acre and their graves are kept in perpetual care, while the graves of Emmet's men are in wilderness. Even the grave of Murrough, though marked by a stone, has never been attended to. In 1760, General Dilke tried to turn Bully's Acre into a botanical gardens but the men from the Liberties soon put a stop to that. They came at night-time and pulled down the walls to protect their family graves. The name Bully's Acre is a corruption of the word *bayl, baily* or *bailiff,* and not from tough Dubliners as some people think.

Across the road, where the houses meet near the railway bridge, stood St John's Well. It was reputed to have curative waters and the people of Dublin came in pilgrimage to it on St John's feast-day. St John's Stations became very popular, too popular in fact, for a certain element used to mix ale and spirits with water from the holy well and sit there drinking it all day. Soon riots broke out and the Irish House of Commons passed an Act in 1710 threatening fines, whipping at The Royal Exchange and imprisonment for anyone found in a drunken manner at St John's Well. This notice was posted all over Dublin and soon the drinkers stopped coming to the well. However, the pilgrimages continued up to about the year 1800.

Beyond the site of this well was an inn where Emmet and Denis Lambert Redmond had breakfast on the morning of 23 July, 1803. They were here to have a last look at the Artillery Barracks in Islandbridge, which was to have been attacked that evening. While they were eating, the tavern owner, Nasan Browne, was running down Kilmainham to Dublin Castle to inform the Chief Secretary that he had seen Redmond, whom he knew was a rebel, watching the sentry on the Artillery Barracks. It was in this barracks that John Boyle O'Reilly, the Fenian, was stationed. He was a member of the 10th Hussars and had recruited several members of the British forces into the Fenian ranks. If you hear the sound of drums as you pass the barrack-gate, it is probably the echo of O'Reilly's drum-head court-martial. Here in the valley of two hills, facing the British War memorial, is where Irish patriots came to plan attacks in 1803, 1867 and 1916.

The first hill, to the left, leads to Sarah Bridge and the swinging gates of the Phoenix Park. Sarah was the wife of the Duke of Westmoreland, Viceroy of Ireland, and they say the bridge was built in her name and honour to give her a short-cut to her beloved fields in Kilmainham. The Liffey here is a noted place for fishing. The hill to the right takes us back by St John's Well and Bully's Acre to Kilmainham Jail and Major Sirr's Stag House. The office of a chocolate company stands today where the Major stood among his informers and spies. The Stag House was a type of prison where unfortunate people were held by Sirr. Many of the law-breakers found themselves doing an informer's job in order to get a few weeks' leave from the Stag House and the Major's clutches. Across the road is Kilmainham Jail, where many Irish Republicans met their end. From 1797 to 1923, it was the symbol of British terror in Ireland. Go in and see the haunted cell, Anne Devlin's doorway, the execution yard and the museum. And take a good look at Grace Gifford's 'Kilmainham Madonna' painted on the wall of a cell.

Gipsy Rose Lee, a colourful character who was a Romany Prince and dressed in beautiful gipsy clothes, lived nearby. I can see him now, standing at the corner of Lady Lane, hands on hips, head in the air and his scarlet sash blowing in the wind. In memory, I revisit the fancy fair, with its swing-boats, hoop-la stalls, ghost train and Gipsy Rose Lee telling fortunes from his caravan home. The road to the left leads to Inchicore and the road to the right goes down to Mount Brown Hill where the boundary of old Kilmainham ends, beside the cottage where Liam Mellows once lived. Mellows was executed in Mountjoy Jail on 8 December 1922.

St Stephen's Green in 1873.

CHAPTER 6

THE CITY CENTRE

ST STEPHEN'S GREEN

DUBLIN'S MAGNIFICENT SQUARE, known as 'The Green', has thirteen avenues radiating from it, one more than from the Arc de Triomphe in Paris. They are: South King Street, Grafton Street, Dawson Street, Kildare Street, Merrion Row, Hume Street, Leeson Street, Earlsfort Terrace, Harcourt Street, Cuffe Street, Proud's Lane, York Street and Glover's Alley.

Walk up and down the thirteen avenues and if you get tired, pop into the Green, feed the ducks, sit in the sun on one of the seats or on the wall of O'Connell Bridge. Yes, we have two O'Connell Bridges in Dublin. After your rest, take a walk around the Green itself. Keep to the parkside among the trees and look across the road. From here you will get an excellent view of the many historic houses and buildings around the square.

Start at the corner of Grafton Street. Number 3 was the old Dublin Bread Company, the DBC, where Pearse and McDonagh had their morning tea and scones. Number Six housed the offices of the Royal Society of Antiquarians of Ireland. Their volumes and journals can be studied in the National Library and at their headquarters in Merrion Square. They contain a mine of information on Dublin and Ireland. The National Literary Society also met in the same house.

Number 16 was at one time the palace of the Protestant Archbishop of Dublin. The Bishops Beresford and Magee spent a fortune on the interior decorations of this house. When Richard Whateley became Archbishop and took up residence in 1831, he threatened to whitewash the beautiful hallway and staircase. Richard didn't go down too well with the swanks of Dublin but he was a true friend of the poor and the needy. In the evenings he used to sit on the steps of his house, smoking a long, cheap clay pipe. He also played with the children of the city in the Green and was never without his three mongrel dogs. For thirty-two years, he was the most noted and colourful figure in St Stephen's Green.

The Shelbourne Hotel stands on the site of Lord Shelbourne's residence. This gentleman was a descendant of the Fitzmaurice who came over with Strongbow and became lord and master in Ireland. They robbed 100,000 acres in Kerry and several thousands of acres in other counties. The Shelbournes also owned lands just outside Inchicore and areas like Robinhood, the Fox and Geese, Bluebell and Red Cow all belonged to his Lordship. These tracts of land were all part of the manor of Drimnagh.

Number 72 was the home of 'The Sham Squire', a notorious informer on the '98 heroes. Mr Francis Higgins got this nickname by pretending he was a relation of Lord Clonmel and marrying a rich merchant's daughter. He was soon found out and his new wife fled. Higgins had started as a shoe-black and later had a small huckster shop in a basement near Green Street court-house. He died in 1806. Oliver St John Gogarty lived for a time in Number 32. The old St Vincent's Hospital stood on the site of Grattan's house and was the residence of the Earl of Meath. The hospital has now moved out to Elm Park and the original 18th century facade is reproduced on part of the new site.

THE CITY CENTRE

Iveagh House, now occupied by the Department of Foreign Affairs, was the home of Sir Benjamin Lee Guinness, the 'Porter King' who saved St Patrick's Cathedral from ruin. Watch out when you're passing Number 86 or Buck Whaley might land on your back. Buck is said to have jumped from a window and landed on a passing coach. He was one of the kings of the Hell Fire Club and for a bet of £10,000 he travelled all the way to Jerusalem, played handball on the walls of the Holy City and then made his way back again. After this he was known as Jerusalem Whaley. One of his favourite places was Daly's Club at Number 17 College Green.

A strange number in St Stephen's Green was 94½, the official number of Wesley College. The quaint old red-brick building and the little chapel have gone. They stood way in off the square almost as if they were playing a game

Wesley College, St Stephen's Green, which has since been demolished.

of hiding. It is sad that Wesley is no longer there, because it gave that side of the Green a little bit more character and charm. Number 110 was Epworth House, a residence for Wesley College girls. Number 112 is the Unitarian Church, known to generations of Dubliners as the Damer Hall, the home of actors, actresses and playwrights. Some of Brendan Behan's plays first saw the light of day here. It is noted for plays in Gaelic. Kapp and Peterson, the famous pipe manufacturers, occupied Number 113.

The Royal College of Surgeons is worthy of a special visit. This is where the sack-'em-ups came with the bodies stolen from graveyards. The College has a magnificent history which would fill many volumes. Sir Charles Cameron, an ex-President, wrote a book giving a detailed account of Dublin's early medical and surgical days. The College history goes back to the days of the red-and-white poles, when the surgeons and barbers were all one body. In those days, you could get your hair cut and your gallstones out at the same time and by the same practitioner. Later, however, the surgeons disowned the barbers, and the only relic the barbers have today is their red-and-white pole. The College was taken over in 1916 by Commandant Mallin with the Countess Markievicz and the Irish Citizen Army.

All the buildings beyond the College of Surgeons have been pulled down to make way for the Stephen's Green shopping centre. One of these houses, Number 124, was the birthplace of Robert Emmet. Its demolition is a sad reflection on the memory of one of our noble patriots. His statue stands opposite the College outside the Green railings, not far from the monument of Lord Ardilaun, the man who gave the poor of Dublin St Stephen's Green.

Study the old bye-laws governing behaviour in the Green. You couldn't smoke, curse, chase girls, court, bring your dog, stay after dark etc. Each gate had its own key and a person living on the Green was the Key-Custodian. At

THE CITY CENTRE

one time, only the gentry were allowed to walk on its parks, but Lord Ardilaun changed all that. The poor of Dublin made a collection among themselves to put up the monument to this generous man.

The first avenue we visit is South King Street. Here is the Gaiety Theatre, started in November 1871 by the Gunn Brothers. They also sold pianos in Grafton Street. The Gunn family kept the theatre going for many years and it was the late Jimmy O'Dea and Harry O'Donovan who put the Gaiety on the map of the world theatre. The old gods (the gallery) are long gone but can you remember the days of opera at ninepence a seat and the singing by the audience during the interval? This theatre saw many famous names, great stars, happy moments, tears of laughter, the spotlight, the orchestral music. Jimmy O'Dea led his one-man show until Maureen Potter came

The south side of St Stephen's Green, showing the former Centenary Church on the left, then the gates to what was Wesley College. On the corner, further down is the former Russell Hotel.

along (See chapter 'The Comedy King').

South King Street ends at the wall of Mercer's Hospital, the ancient site of St Stephen's Hospital for Lepers, from which the Green gets its name. Founded in 1224 by Dublin Corporation, the hospital bordered the lands of the Archbishop's Liberty of St Sepulchre's and it has a chequered history. Cromwell took it over as a military barracks in 1649 and, by the year 1698, the hospital, a church, three castles and stone houses around it were all in ruins. A quarter of a century later, Miss Mary Mercer built a house for twenty sick girls. This was the foundaation of Mercer's Hospital which operated on this site for over 750 years. The hospital is no longer in use and the building is now used as Health Board offices.

The second avenue is Grafton Street. Samuel Whyte's Academy stood where Bewley's famous coffee-house and restaurant stand today. At the corner of Chatham Street, Wolfe Tone fell in love. Matilda Witherington, a beautiful sixteen-year-old, was looking out of the window of her Grafton Street home as Tone was on his way to St Stephen's Green.

At the corner of South Anne Street, the informer Armstrong met John and Henry Sheares, whom he later betrayed and caused to be sent to Newgate gallows side-by-side. At the corner of Duke Street, the Fenian James Coady dropped his dagger while trying to kill an informer. He tried to escape through Johnston's Court but was arrested in Clarendon Street and sentenced to twenty years' penal servitude in an English dungeon. After his release, he went to Australia and became the leader of Republican opinion in support of the Irish cause.

Just beyond the corner of Harry Street is McDaid's pub, the meeting-place of Brendan Behan, Patrick Kavanagh and the poets and writers of Dublin. The corner beyond McDaid's leads to Balfe Street, formerly Pitt Street. The

THE CITY CENTRE

composer Michael Balfe was born at Number 10. Balfe wrote *The Bohemian Girl* and the immortal ballads, 'When Other Lips' and 'I dreamt I Dwelt in Marble Halls'.

The Balfes were a very musical family and Michael learned his first notes from his father, who was an accomplished violinist. Balfe's works became known all over the world and he is one of the few Dublin composers whose music and lyrics have been translated into German, French, Russian and Italian. He received many honours and was made a Chevalier of the Legion d'Honneur in Paris. He died on 20 October 1869, at the age of sixty-one. My mother's favourite musical was always *The Bohemian Girl*. But, then, I suppose she was clannish. She, too, was born in Number 10 Pitt Street.

If you see a crowd of men at the corner of Wicklow Street, maybe they are on their way to the Barbers' Hall at Number 25. The men have urgent business. Their chief, James Stephens, is in Richmond Jail and a new Fenian leader and military council has to be decided on. Colonel Kelly will get the chief's position. He was the man who led the raid at the smashing of the van in Manchester. The same house was also a secret meeting-place of the 1848 leaders.

The third avenue is Dawson Street. St Ann's Church is where Wolfe Tone was married to the young girl from Grafton Street. It is noted for its lunchtime music, lectures and poetry. The parish dates from 1707 and is built on land presented by Joshua Dawson. The poet Felicia Hemans is buried in the vaults. Sir Hugh Lane, founder of the Municipal Gallery, loved St Ann's and might have been buried here had he not drowned at sea with the *Lusitania*.

The Mansion House, the Lord Mayor's residence, is noted for its Round, Oak and Supper Rooms. Here, from October to Christmas, sales of work, with bargains galore, book stalls, wheels of fortune, all in aid of worthy causes, are held. Horse Show week brings the Antique Fair, where you can buy treasures of golden days, priceless objects, some of which a few years ago were only junk and scrap. Look out for prints of Dublin, books, furniture, silverware, old lamps, maps, coins and the glitter and dust of centuries.

Number 19 is the Royal Irish Academy, where you will find a treasure of books and where lectures and afternoon meetings are held. It has many historic associations with Dublin city. I studied a lot of Dublin's history in the Academy and had, in fact, made several visits before they realised I was not a member. Even when they discovered me among a mountain of Dublin books and maps, they allowed me to continue and suggested that I get a member to propose me for membership. When I saw the list of members headed by all my political enemies, I decided to go back to Dean Armstrong and Marsh's Library, where I could come and go with more comfort.

The fourth avenue is Kildare Street, where Charles Dickens's son went for his two bottles of whiskey. And the drop he got from Mitchell's at Number 21 was so bloody good that he sat down after drinking it and wrote them a letter. That was on 24 December, 1877. Charles's son, also named Charles, got his

On the left is the Molesworth Hall and in the centre St Ann's school. This fine row of 19th century buildings stood in Molesworth Street, but were demolished in the seventies.

THE CITY CENTRE

two bottles for thirty bob. Some of the house numbers have been altered over the years.

Bram Stoker, the author of *Dracula*, lived at Number 30 from 1847 to 1912. He was also a theatre manager and wrote several other books, including a few romantic novels. The one written for his wife was called *Pretty Polly is a Dinger*.

Number 38 was the home of Mrs Butler, the widow who sheltered the Fenian chief, James Stephens, after his escape from Richmond Jail. Stephens later went to France. Mrs Butler went down in the world (some say due to her Fenian sympathies) and died a pauper in Ballybough. Number Thirty-Nine was the home of Lady Morgan. It was a long journey with the jug of porter from Bride Street. I wonder did she spill any or have a few sips on the way.

Leinster House was originally the residence of the Fitzgerald family, the Earls of Kildare. It was Lord Edward who said: 'Leinster House does not inspire bright ideas.' The building was started in 1745 and today it is hard to credit that a building of this scale was erected for one family. In 1815 it was sold to the RDS and later in 1922 the Irish Free State took it over. On the right of Leinster House is the National Museum, which contains a fabulous collection of Celtic and Viking ornaments and thousands of other items. On the left, facing it, is our grossly overcrowded National Library and, hidden beside it, the National College of Art, once the servant quarters of Leinster House.

The Kildare Street Club has lost a lot of its dignity and the tram conductor can no longer crack his daily joke as the tram stopped at the corner: 'Tell Carhampton I'll be late for lunch.' Here in bygone days one could find bowler hats, pin-stripes, umbrellas and walrus moustaches and hear about the 'Thin Red Line' with stories of India, the Boxer Rising and Victorian days. Later,

ME JEWEL AND DARLIN' DUBLIN

*The Kildare Street Club after it was opened in 1861.
The view is from Trinity College.*

in Black-and-Tan days, there would be talk of Sam Browne belts, gold braid, raincoats, slouch hats and flashing revolvers.

The fifth avenue is Merrion Row. It is quite short and you'll almost pass it by. Go slowly and watch out for the Huguenot graveyard. The grave-stones still bear their exotic names. Raise your hat to their memory, their skills, their honest dealings. They were the French men and women who came to Dublin, found a home and became more Dublin than Dubliners themselves. The road ahead leads to Gallows Cross at the corner of Fitzwilliam Street. It was here that Archbishop Dermot O'Hurley was hanged in 1584. He was betrayed by a man called Walter Ball, who also betrayed his own mother for sheltering the Archbishop. O'Donoghue's public-house in Merrion Row is famous for characters, ballads and booze. This is where Ronnie Drew, Luke Kelly and

THE CITY CENTRE

the Dubliners started and where new Dublin characters are born every night.

Number 18 Baggot Street was the home of the D'Olier family of silversmiths, one of whom was Lord Mayor of Dublin. They left their name on one of our streets and many of their priceless masterpieces of gold and silver are in the National Museum and in private collections. Number 67 is the house where Thomas Osborne Davis died and Number 128 is the house where the Sheares brothers were arrested in 1798.

> 'If we live influenced by wind and sun and tree, and not by the passions and deeds of the past, we are a thriftless and a hopeless people. From a knowledge of local history comes that permanent and proud nationality which appears to sacrifice life and wealth to liberty, but really wins all together. This country of ours is no sand-bank thrown up by some recent caprice of earth. It is an ancient land, honoured in the archives of civilisation, traceable into antiquity by its piety, its valour, and its sufferings.'
>
> *Thomas Davis, Young Irelander*

The sixth avenue is Hume Street. Here is located Hume Street Hospital which deals with all kinds of skin disorders. Around the corner, in Ely Place, was the home of Oliver St John Gogarty. Could that be James Joyce I see looking out the window? He seems to be smiling. Has Gogarty really given him permission to write the book? 'I don't care a damn what you say of me,' said Gogarty, 'as long as it is literature.' But then, when *Ulysses* appeared in 1922, Gogarty had other words to say: 'That bloody Joyce, whom I kept in my youth, has written a book you can read on all the lavatory walls of Dublin.'

Number 4 Ely Place was the town residence of John Philpot Curran. In Number 6 lived Lord Clare, one of the most hated men in Ireland. He was Attorney-General in 1798 and was responsible for the execution of the rebel leaders. Many times this house was stormed by the citizens of Dublin.

Ely House is today the headquarters of the Knights of St Columbanus. It is one of the finest Georgian houses in Dublin and the inner hallway, staircase and ceilings are magnificent. Visitors are allowed at reasonable hours.

The seventh avenue is Leeson Street, which leads to the gateway of Dublin. This was the Royal Way along which the Kings, Queens and Viceroys of England entered the city. At Leeson Street Bridge the addresses of welcome were read. Halfway up the street, turn into Pembroke Street Upper and cast a glance at Number 14, the lodging-house of Edward Duffy, Rossa's friend, who was arrested here and sentenced to fifteen years in an English dungeon. On a Sunday morning in Millbank Jail, many miles across the sea from Pembroke street, O'Donovan Rossa heard the words, whispered through the ventilator in his cell door: 'Duffy is dead, Duffy is dead.' Rossa could not sleep that night and as he twisted and turned on his wooden plank bed, he wrote a poem in his mind for Edward Duffy. One of the verses goes like this:

The gloomy way is brightened when
   We walk with those we love;
The heavy-load is lightened when we
   Bear and they approve.
The path of life grows darker to
   Me as I journey on,
For the truest hearts that travelled it
   Are falling one by one.

The eighth avenue is Earlsfort Terrace, for many years the home of University College Dublin, the old Alexandra College and the C.D.S. or Clergy's Daughters' Schools. Now all three have been relocated, U.C.D. to Belfield and Alexandra College and the C.D.S. to Milltown. The former University

THE CITY CENTRE

buildings now house the National Concert Hall and offices have been built where the other two schools stood. For several generations this had been a terrace of education for the rich, leading out to Adelaide Road, where the Eye and Ear Hospital is sited. A Presbyterian church frames the end of the street and further down Adelaide Road is St Finian's, the German Lutheran Church.

The ninth avenue is Harcourt Street. Number 22 was the residence of Leonard McNally, the Crown informer in the days of Emmet. Numbers 15 and 16 were the home of 'Copper Face Jack', John Scott, Earl of Clonmel. He was the judge who tried the Rev. Mr Jackson, who committed suicide in the dock, but Clonmel still insisted that he be brought to his feet so that he could be sentenced to death.

Next door in Number 14 lived Sir Jonah Barrington. Jonah's wife had a habit of looking out the side-window into the Earl's garden. The Earl made a smart remark to Jonah about his prurient wife. Jonah was so furious that he called in a team of masons and had the window blocked up. It has now been re-opened and you can see it in the adjoining laneway. Jonah was a friend of the Sheares Brothers and he voted against the Act of Union in 1800.

Number 6 Harcourt Street was the home of Cardinal Newman. It was also the headquarters of Sinn Féin and, if you could imagine a small man on the roof, it would be Joe Clarke, the caretaker, watching for Black-and-Tans to pass so that Collins, Boland and Brugha could get safely away.

Number 40 was the High School, founded by Erasmus Smith, where George Bernard Shaw and W.B. Yeats got their early education. This school is still with us but has moved out of town. The beautiful railway station, which once provided the terminal for the Bray via Dundrum line, is now part of Findlater's Wines Ltd. They have a superb museum under the archway, which is well worth a visit. The old Court Laundry which stood nearby is gone.

ME JEWEL AND DARLIN' DUBLIN

Do you remember the lovely laundry vans painted primrose and white, with their well-groomed horses, polished brasses and black oiled leather harness? Many a year they made their way to the R.D.S. Horse Show to collect winners' ribbons and cups. My old van in the White Heather livery was always like a tramp beside them. One day I remarked on this to my van man. He snarled at me and said: 'We don't go in for washing vans, we go in for washing clothes.' Nevertheless, the Court Laundry vans added glamour and dignity to the streets of Dublin.

The tenth avenue is Cuffe Street. The house I miss most is Mr Coppolo's ice-cream parlour. He was the king of ice-cream in Dublin. Some people made ice-cream from condensed milk mixed with water and it tasted like cornflour. Coppolo's ice-cream (Lord rest him!) had a flavour I couldn't describe. The penny wafers were as thick as your head. They were only gorgeous!

At one time, this small street had four pawn-shops. One of them was in the back kitchen of Number 47. Dean Walter Blake Kirwan, the Jesuit who went over to the other side, lived here. He was a powerful preacher and when he gave a charity sermon the ladies and gents filled the plates with their gold rings, jewellery, tie pins, cuff-links etc. Sometimes, this was only for show. Next day they would call to Cuffe Street to redeem the items for a few shillings, saying that they fell into the plate accidentally. The last of the four pawn-shops was knocked down some years back, along with the Bricklayers' Hall and the street has never looked the same since. All its character seems to have disappeared.

The pawnshop in Number 48 Cuffe Street was previously named Meredith & Co. It was owned by a Mr Edward Sheridan of Sandymount in 1917. Next door was the headquarters of the Ancient Guild of Incorporated Brick and Stonelayers' Trade Unions, which was one of the oldest Guilds in Dublin,

THE CITY CENTRE

with a long and coloured history. In 1795, its members stopped work on Gandon's Custom House in protest against stone-masons being brought over from England. This was a time that Dublin was full of craftsmen in stone and brick. Stone-laying in bygone days was a fine art job, as can be seen by the old walls at St Audoen's, Christ Church and Dublin Castle. Cuffe Street was also a meeting-place for the Irish Invincibles in 1882.

The eleventh avenue is Proud's Lane. Can you see two men in green-and-grey uniforms, with short Mauser rifles, looking into the yard of Beverley Smith's to see if they can commandeer the large furniture removal vans to use as a barricade? This happened during the 1916 Rising.

The twelfth avenue is York Street, where Clarence Mangan worked as a clerk to a solicitor. He later lived for a time at Number 6. Mangan fell in love with Margaret Stackpoole from Ranelagh. She led him on to the day he bought the ring and let him propose before telling him she was already married. Mangan went home to write 'The Nameless One' and then took to the drink. He later contracted fever and was found dying in a cellar in Bride Street. He died in the Meath Hospital in 1849.

The best-known house in York Street was Number 41, 'The Workmen's Club'.

The Dublin Total Abstinence League, whose motto was 'Ireland sober, Ireland Free,' the people who, according to Brendan Behan, 'would only speak Irish but wouldn't drink Irish'. It was a mecca for IRA men in Black-and-Tan days. The Christmas draws provided great excitement. It was only three pence for a ticket and there were nearly a hundred prizes, including turkeys, hampers, wine, cakes and five-pound notes. The best value in raffle tickets at Christmas was always at the Workmen's Club. 'Keep me two, Missus. I'll see ya, Saturday. Don't let them go now. Saturday …' Many a poor family dined like kings on a Christmas Day, thanks to the Workmen's Club. The ticket itself was worth the threepence. It was a large piece of coloured paper with a serial number in the top corner and every prize listed. Also included were the closing date, day of the draw, newspaper notice and the latest time to claim your winnings.

A building very much in use in York Street today is the Salvation Army men's hostel. Here a man can find a bed for the night, sit and relax in the television room and also enjoy a meal in the restaurant, all at modest prices. Most of the old buildings in this street have been demolished, but the Salvation Army continue their long tradition here and at their other centres around the city. The 'Sally Ann', as the Dubliners called them, were always held in very high esteem.

The thirteenth avenue is Glovers' Alley which runs along the side of the College of Surgeons. It was often used by Robert Emmet on his way home from school. In 1917, the gentry came here to make use of the Turkish baths which stood between two mineral water manufacturing companies, Hovenden Orr and the Irish Direct Trading Company. At the end of the alley is the factory of Smith and Sheppard, the old-established firm who manufacture artificial limbs and surgical instruments. Fannin & Co., which at one time had their premises in nearby Grafton Street, were also a very old, established company in the same business. It is nice to remember that Dublin manufacturers were experts in this type of work in the early days of surgical aids.

And so we end our tour of the Green and its thirteen avenues.

TRINITY COLLEGE

ON MY FIRST DAY AT WORK in Switzer's of Grafton Street, I was sent with a parcel to Trinity College. I came out of the laneway into Wicklow Street and

The front gates of Trinity College, facing College Green.

started to walk up towards George's Street. It suddenly dawned on me that I didn't know where Trinity College was. Near the top of Exchequer Street, I asked a policeman. He sent me down Dame Court and told me to turn right and that it was the large building stretching across the street. He also shouted after me that there were two statues in front of it, one looking out and the other looking in. As I came closer to the College, I examined the address label and wondered what was inside. It read: 'With care. Fragile. Mr T.L. Wilkins, Junior Fellow, T.C.D.' Then I began to notice the College, the small window panes, the pillars, the way it stood in the centre of the street, the clock and flagpole. Then I started counting the windows – 43, 44, 45 – and then I bumped into a lamp-post!

I stood at the statue of Grattan and gazed like a tourist. Another look at Burke and Goldsmith before I passed in by the open wicket door in the archtype gateway. The gateman sat in his little office on the left. His desk was

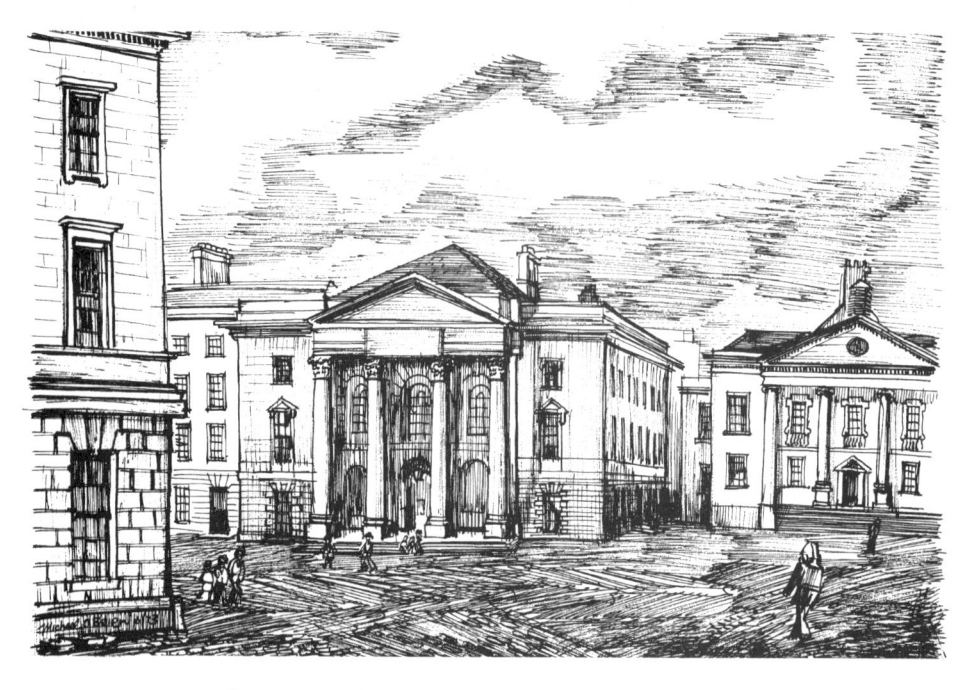

Looking across Parliament Square at the chapel of Trinity College.

filled with papers, books, wire clips and dozens of door keys. He was dressed in a navy-blue swallow-tail coat and a black cap like those I saw in Tyson's window. He examined the label and gave me directions. As I went through the dark, dimly-lit hallway, I saw the scores of notices – 'Lost and Found'; 'Room wanted'; 'Divinity books for sale'; 'Meeting tonight'; 'Dance in the Boat Club' and a Thought for the Day which read: 'Very few of us get dizzy from doing good turns.' I could have stopped there all day reading. I crossed the cobble-stoned Parliament Square, peeped into the chapel and the Examination Hall and gave the same attention and gaze to the campanile as I had done to Grattan outside the gate.

I could see the rows of books behind the Library window and now and again a face appeared. Another black-caped swallow-tail-coated man passed

THE CITY CENTRE

me by and then I saw an elderly grey-haired clergyman who looked rather odd in his light-brown buttoned gaiters, his blackthorn walking stick with a silver top and a thick gold watch-chain across his green-coloured waistcoat. The clergyman suddenly called out: 'Skip, skip.' I thought he was talking to me. 'Beg your pardon, sir,' I said. 'The skip, the skip,' he said, pointing after the man in the black cap. I put my fingers into my mouth and gave a loud whistle which echoed all over the quiet College grounds. The skip turned and noticed the waving blackthorn stick and came running back. By the look on his face, I think he thought the clergyman had given the whistle signal. The old 'skip' tradition in Trinity died when the last one was buried. I moved along fast and found the address I was looking for.

On my way back out, I read a few more notices in the hallway, gave the gateman a 'thank you' salute which he returned with a smile and I gave another salute to Grattan which he didn't return at all! That was the first of a thousand parcels I delivered to Trinity College, to the Provost's house, the G.M.B. (Graduate Memorial Building), the School of Divinity, the Senior Fellows, the Junior Fellows and a few students who were called Junior and Senior Freshmen and Junior and Senior Sophisters.

I can recall the College rag-days when the students dressed up in all sorts of gear, and some with hardly any gear, kissing girls, letting the air out of bicycle wheels, stopping trams and motors, doing point-duty in a pair of pyjamas. They held parades with floats through the streets of Dublin and carried on with every type of behaviour that was unbecoming of Trinity boys. The Provost put down his boot and the rag days were banned. Despite the behaviour of the students, the Dublin people loved the rag days and the money collected always went to a deserving charity.

The Archbishop of Dublin, Adam Loftus, was the man responsible for getting the Charter from Queen Elizabeth and the land from the Lord Mayor and the people of Dublin. In fact, the Lord Mayor, Thomas Smith, laid the foundation-stone on 13 April, 1592, and the College doors opened for students on 9 January, 1593. For four hundred years, the College has been the principal University of the nation. Dean Swift, Edmund Burke, Oliver Goldsmith, Grattan, Tone, Emmet, Moore, Davis and a host of other famous names passed through its gateway since then. The name on the Royal Charter read:

> 'The Provost, Fellows and Scholars of the Holy and Undivided Trinity of Queen Elizabeth near Dublin.'

The College site was originally the old Augustinian monastery of All Hallows or All Saints, which was built in 1166 by Dermot MacMurrough, King of Leinster. The dissolved monastery of All Hallows was granted to the citizens of Dublin in 1534 for their loyal support and for losses sustained during the rebellion of Silken Thomas, son of the Earl of Kildare.

The greatest treasure of the College is the Book of Kells, often referred to as the most beautified testimony to the Christian faith. It can be seen in the new Colonnades under its armour-plated glass. In 1953, it was bound into four volumes for greater protection for the generations unborn. Every year, more than a quarter of a million people from all over the world visit the College to see it. The Book of Kells is the work of the monks of St Columba, an Irish saint who went to Iona in 563 A.D. with twelve followers and converted half of Scotland and Northern England to Christianity. Early in the ninth century, the followers of the saint decided to produce a book more beautiful than any other. The skins of one hundred and fifty calves provided the smooth vellum leaves. The colours used by the illuminators came from plants and flowers.

THE CITY CENTRE

Four chief artists, assisted by several other monks, spent a lifetime on their labour of love.

In 806, the Vikings raided Iona and killed sixty-eight monks at Martyr's Bay. During the raid, the artist-monks escaped with their book across the sea to Ireland and were given refuge at Kells, Co. Meath. Here, the book was completed and remained on display in Kells for nearly two hundred years. The Annals of Ulster record: 'The chief relic of the Western World was wickedly stolen in the night in the year 1006.' The thieves buried the book and it was discovered a few months later. In the 12th century, the book was in the care of the Bishop of Meath, where it was venerated as the great Gospel Book of St Columba. Henry Jones, Scoutmaster-General to Cromwell, became Bishop of Meath in 1661 and presented The Book of Kells to Trinity College. Other treasures in the College are The Book of Durrow, The Book of Armagh, The Garland of Howth, The Book of Leinster, the Spanish Organ, the Brian Boru Harp and thousands of rare, priceless antiquarian books in the library. Under the Copyright Act, Trinity gets a free copy of every book published in Ireland and Britain.

King James II used the College as a military barracks in 1689 and it was he who appointed its first Catholic Provost, the Rev. Michael Moore. The second Catholic Provost is the present Thomas Mitchell. Trinity was the first College to grant degrees to Jews and women. In the years 1724-1855, Professors of Language and Literature taught Greek, Latin, English, Irish, German, Hebrew, Arabic, Persian, Hindustani and Romantic languages.

In the year 1785, Provost Francis Andrews endowed the Astronomical Observatory at Dunsink, Castleknock, which was placed by statute in 1791 under the management of the Royal Astronomer of Ireland. The Ballast Office clock, which used to be at the corner of Westmoreland Street, was always right according to Dubliners because it was controlled by an electric current transmitted each second by a time-clock in the Observatory. A few clocks in Trinity College were also controlled by the same system.

The West Front building dates from 1752 and was designed by Keane and Sanderson. In 1759, the Provost's House was built by an Irish architect, John Smyth, who copied, and changed in parts, Lord Burlington's design of a London house. The chapel was designed by Sir William Chambers in 1787 and cost £22,000 to build. The campanile, which replaced the old belfry, was the gift of the Primate, Lord George Beresford, in 1852.

Trinity College stretches from the front gate at College Green to the back gate at Lincoln Place. The area takes in one side of Pearse Street down to Westland Row corner and then runs along one side of Westland Row, where Oscar Wilde was born, and up to the corner of Lincoln Place. Most of the buildings inside this perimeter have been acquired by the College, with the exception of a few. Trinity has become a city within a city in the heart of Dublin. As each day passes, new buildings and extensions continue. Students come from all over the world to study at the University of Dublin. James Joyce said that Trinity was a dull stone. I beg to differ, Mr Joyce, Trinity is one of the brightest jewels in the city of Dublin!

AROUND COLLEGE GREEN

'EXCUSE ME, SIR,' THE GENTLE VOICE SAID. 'Could you show us the way to the old Irish Parliament House?' I turned around and saw a group of teenage girls. Tourists, no doubt, with rucksacks, tin mugs, kettles, black boots, coloured jeans and heavy woollen jumpers. Blondes, brunettes and even a red-head, all smiling, with maps and brochures in their hands. The gentle voice told me that I was in the company of New Zealand school-teachers who

THE CITY CENTRE

College Green with the statue of Grattan.

were on a tour of Europe. This was their first visit to Dublin. I couldn't resist the temptation to give an instant tour!

'I'll take you there myself,' I said, and suddenly I was surrounded by the pretty group. The maps and brochures were stuck into rucksacks and out came the notebooks and pens. 'Spell that, please.' 'What date did you say?' 'What street is that?' 'That's D'Olier Street, a good Huguenot name, a sheriff of Dublin. Did you ever hear of Samuel Lover, the writer and artist? Well, he lived in Number 9 D'Olier Street. He's the man who wrote the story of Rory O'Moore, the leader of the 1641 Rising. The battle-cry in those days was: 'For God, Ireland and Rory O'Moore.' 'Where's the Red Bank restaurant?' one girl asked. 'Beside you,' I said, 'but they don't serve food today. They serve Mass instead. Now it's the Chapel of The Blessed Sacrament Fathers.' I don't think that they were all R.C.s but in they went to light candles and say a quiet prayer. As I stood in the entry, I wondered what Joyce or Gogarty would say if they could see the shrines and pews on the floor of the Red Bank.

We walked across by Fleet Street, the birthplace of Kevin Barry. They had heard the ballad and one of them hummed it quietly as we passed the offices of *The Irish Times*, the oldest daily newspaper in Ireland, founded in 1859. I told them the story of old Mr Smylie who refused to print his paper with the new-fangled machinery and stuck to the old method for many years because he did not wish to make a large number of type-setters redundant. I told them, also, of the 'Sinn Féin Rebellion Handbook' that *The Irish Times* printed after the 1916 Rising. It cost one shilling and sixpence then. Today it's £20 or more in the second-hand bookshops of Dublin. They say in Dublin: 'If you miss the *Irish Times*, you miss part of the day and if you go into the Pearl Bar, you'll miss the whole bloody day!' The Pearl was the writers' Paradise where you could find Roddy the Rover,

THE CITY CENTRE

Myles na gCopaleen, James Plunkett, Brendan Behan and Patrick Kavanagh looking for 'wan lousy word' to finish his poem. It was the boozing place of journalists, copy-boys, compositors, actors and artists.

'Come across the street, girls,' I said, 'and view the Parliament in three dimensions. The Ionic columns were designed by Edward Lovett Pearse who died before his beautiful building was completed. Around the corner, the Corinthian pillars were designed by James Gandon and the Foster Place pillars by Robert Parke.' We stood at the statue of Thomas Osborne Davis and the girls giggled at the Omo suds and bubbles in the waters of the fountain beside it. 'The students,' I said, 'and it's not even a rag-day.'

Parliament House is today the Bank of Ireland, which moved there from Mary's Abbey in 1802. For £40,000 they purchased the finest building of its kind in the world. Perhaps it was sold to a Bank to prevent others from making political speeches in its chambers. Maybe they were afraid that the golden words spoken against the Act of Union of 1800 in the House of Lords still lingered around the Dublin glass chandelier made by Chesby's glass-house in Ballybough and that the spirit of the words would inspire others to re-establish the independent Parliament. The windowless building is adorned by the statues of Wisdom, Justice, Liberty, Hibernia, Fidelity and Commerce, sculptured by Edward Smyth.

Sir Arthur Chichester, Cromwell's man who planned the Plantation of Ulster, leased his house to the Irish Parliament in 1661. The present building was started in 1729. The Westmoreland Street front dates from 1785 and the Foster Place front from 1787. The total cost was more than £95,000. Foster Place gets its name from John Foster, the last speaker in the old Irish Parliament or 'Grattan's Parliament' as some historians call it. The Bank porter told us that his uniform of red, blue and yellow was the same colour as the colours worn by the Parliament staff in days gone by. He showed us King William crossing the Boyne and the Siege of Derry woven in beautiful wall-length tapestries, the silver mace of the House of Commons, the glass chandelier and the wood-carved mantlepiece and told us interesting tales of Daly's Club, Jonah Barrington, the duels and the fire-eaters of Dublin who used the statue of St Andrew as a cockshot in target-shooting practice.

The statue stands today, hidden in the yard of St Andrew's Church in Suffolk Street. The New Zealand girls desired to see it and, within a few moments, we were making our way up Church Lane. I told them that St Andrew's stood on ancient land, at one time named the Thingmote, a mound or hill over the town of Dublin where laws were made and robbers hanged. Adam O'Toole was burned at the stake in the year 1327 for daring to say that the Book of Gospels was only fables. We looked for Vanessa's grave in the churchyard but looked in vain. We cleaned the tombstones with our hands to read the names but Vanessa Vanhomrigh's was not among them. I told them the story of how Vanessa died of a broken heart in Turnstile Alley, beside Foster Place and how Stella reared Vanessa's child.

Vanessa was a girl in the life of Dean Swift – a jealous girl who heard of Swift and Stella. She wrote a letter to Stella and spoke of her love for the Dean, asking many pertinent questions. Stella showed the letter to Swift. Mad with rage, he rode to Celbridge where Vanessa was staying, burst in the door, threw down the letter, cursed and raved, cursed and raved again and again, until Vanessa fell in a hysterical and violent manner. For many days, she lay in agony. She would not eat, she would not drink, but wept bitter tears for her loneliness, her foolishness and her unreturned love. She came back to her city residence, broken in health, rejected in love with nothing to live for, not even her child, who was now in other hands. Her grave lies under the roadway in

THE CITY CENTRE

Suffolk Street, beside where McCullough-Pigott's shop used to be. The shop has moved across the street next to St Andrew's Church and you can buy your sheet music there.

St Andrew's Church, which dates from the eleventh century, was originally in Palace Street beside Dublin Castle. In 1670, the Thingmote was levelled and a church built. In 1690 it was used as a prison. The present church, built in 1866, was designed by Lanyon, Lynn and Lanyon of Belfast. St Andrew's is the only Protestant Church in Dublin with a statue of its patron outside its door. I concluded by saying that St Andrew's was the parish church of the old Irish Parliament House. And there I left my new-found friends from New Zealand. As I walked away, I heard their cameras clicking around St Andrew's Church, its bullet-scarred statue and at the centre of the street, the uninscribed tomb of Vanessa Vanhomrigh.

DUBLIN'S REVOLUTIONARY SQUARE

THE ROTUNDA HOSPITAL, previously known as The Lying-in Hospital, is the oldest and the first maternity hospital in the world. From this revolutionary venture in medicine and hospitalisation, involving pre- and post-natal care, came other revolutionary ideas and methods which first saw the light of day beside the Rotunda and around its location in beautiful Parnell Square.

This is the 'Square of the firsts'. Let's walk around it and you will see what I mean. The Rotunda Hospital was founded in 1757 by Dr Bartholomew Mosse, the fifth son of the Rector of Maryborough (now Portlaoise). It was designed by the architect Richard Cassells and completed by his assistant, John Ensor. Mosse was born in Portlaoise and had a very colourful career, travelling widely in Europe before settling in Dublin in 1742. He lived for a while in South Great George's Street, when he was a surgeon in Mercer's Hospital. In 1745, he opened his first hospital in George's Lane, opposite Fade Street, in an old disused theatre. From a small start of six beds, the hospital grew. He continued to convince his friends that the lack of 'lying-in hospitals' was the prime cause of the high death rate in maternity cases.

Soon his idea became the fad of the rich and, as funds poured in, Mosse acquired the site on which the hospital stands today. His life was spent in the service of the poor of Dublin. It was his idea to erect a Round Room and Assembly Hall to raise funds for the hospital from functions, meetings, balls and the like. He did not live to see his plans completed; this was accomplished under his successor, Sir Fielding Ould. Eventually, the Round Room became the Ambassador Cinema and the Assembly Hall became the Gate Theatre, where today you can still see the excellence of Irish drama. Another part of the Assembly Rooms was used in the 1960s and 1970s as the Town and Country Club, where you could dance the night away. It is no longer in use.

Nowadays you don't have to be expecting a baby to go in and visit the Rotunda. Push in the hall-door (at reasonable hours), climb the beautiful staircase designed by Robert West and the door facing you at the top of the stairs leads to the Rotunda chapel, which is a real gem. The plaster-work was carried out by a Frenchman, Bartholomew Carmillion, who came to Dublin and left behind him a masterpiece for generations of Dubliners to admire. Others of his kind came also and, together with craftsmen from Dublin and other parts of Ireland, left us a heritage to admire and wonder at. They had names like Bossi, Adams, Thorpe, Stapleton, West, Kaufman and the Francini Brothers. Read C.P. Curran's book *Dublin Decorative Plasterwork*. It's a treasure in words and pictures.

The Rotunda Round Room was the birthplace of the Irish Volunteers. It was also used by Napper Tandy and the United Irishmen in 1796. From that date

THE CITY CENTRE

onwards, it was the meeting-place of the revolutionaries of 1848, 1867 and 1882, up to the birth of the Sinn Féin organisation on 28 November 1905. Eight years later, a new generation founded another Irish volunteer movement that led to the 1916 Easter Week Rising. The first lecture on 'Socialism and the Irish People' by Robert Owens was also delivered here.

Across the street was Tom Clarke's shop on the corner of Parnell Street and O'Connell Street. Tom Clarke's was the first signature on the Proclamation of 1916. Just beyond the hospital, at the top of Moore Street, Padraig Pearse, the first President of the Provisional Irish Republic, handed over his sword in surrender to General Lowe of the British forces. As the surrender order by Pearse and Connolly was obeyed, the first prisoners laid dotheir arms and weapons at the Parnell Monument and spent their first night in the open prison of the Rotunda Gardens in front of the hospital's main door.

The Gate Theatre was the brainchild of Micheál MacLiammóir and Hilton Edwards. Its two most famous patrons, Lord and Lady Longford, have passed on but I can still remember the gracious Lady adding dignity to the Square as she stood with her collection-box between the two large queues. The 'House Full' signs were up for the cinema and the dance-hall and Lady Longford was aware that her Gate Theatre was half-empty. She always kept the back row of seats, costing only a shilling each, for the hard-up people who wished to enjoy a night at the theatre. Micheál MacLiammóir and Hilton Edwards have also passed on but they are remembered with kindness for their contribution to the theatrical history of Dublin.

As we go around the Square we will call to mind the memories of Richard Kirwan who lived in Number 6 Cavendish Row. Richard was 'The Philosopher of Dublin' in the year 1787 and was a member of the Royal Irish Academy and the Royal Dublin Society. His works came under the subjects of divinity, logic, law, chemistry, geology, metaphysics, mining and several other headings. He was involved in the publication of many books and helped Bunting in his collection of Irish music. He was also the first man in Dublin to offer a reward to his servants for catching flies. He shaved only on a Thursday, the day he allowed ladies to visit him. If anyone overstayed their welcome, Richard would leave the room and come back dressed in his pyjamas and nightcap, with a candle-holder in his hand.

The old Hay Hotel, later Groome's Hotel, got its name from the fact that one of the windows was always open with a supply of hay for the jarveys' and coachmen's horses, while the gentlemen wined and dined. The Hay Hotel provided a twenty-four-hour service.

Number 5 Parnell Square was the birthplace of Oliver St John Gogarty. He was the first man to capture 'the Dublin idiom' – its slang, manners and expressions – in his play *Blight*, several years before Joyce and O'Casey had written their works. Number 9 was the headquarters of Sinn Féin for many years as was Number 16. Number 10 was the Grand Orange Hall of Ireland in 1917. It's a pity that these two neighbours did not make friends during that period. If they had, I'm certain that Ireland today would be a far better and happier country than it is now.

The turn to the right at the Garden Bistro leads to three hotels – the Castle, Barry's and the Belvedere, the last-named being opposite Belvedere College, where Joyce went to school. This is a part of Dublin that feeds half the people of the country on All-Ireland Day at Croke Park.

The Abbey Presbyterian Church, known as Findlater's Church, always has a warm welcome for visitors. It was built in 1864 at the expense of Alexander Findlater, the founder of Dublin's famous grocery, wine and spirits shops. Forty years ago, a fleet of Findlater's lorries delivered all over Ireland, and

O'Connell Street lost a bit of its character when the firm left a few years ago. Its new premises is the old railway station in Harcourt Street. The Writers' Museum beside the church was formerly a Technical School and was once the home of Annie Hutton, the sweetheart of Thomas Davis, the Young Ireland Leader who died in 1845, a few weeks before his wedding day. Their love remains immortal in Davis's ballad 'Annie Dear'.

Number 20 is up for sale at the time of writing. At present, it houses the Banba Hall (National Ballroom) and the offices of the Irish National Union of Vintners', Grocers' and Allied Trades' Assistants. This Union has a proud record of association with the fight for independence. Many of its members made the supreme sacrifice on the scaffold and in the streets of Dublin, the most noted name being Martin Savage who was killed in action during the Black-and-Tan War on the Ashtown Road. Next door is the Municipal Art Gallery. The first of its kind in Europe, it was the town house of John Caulfield, Earl of Charlemont, Commander-in-Chief of the Volunteers of 1782. Charlemont House, which dates from 1763, was designed by Sir William Chambers on the site known as Palace Row. The Earl had his country residence at The Casino, Marino, in Dublin.

The Municipal Art Gallery, or the Hugh Lane Gallery as it used to be known in honour of the founder and the gift of the Hugh Lane collection to the Irish nation, has a wonderful collection of modern art. But you will see here only half of Lane's munificent gift. The other half is in a London gallery. Lane's last wish was for the full collection to remain in Dublin and he added a codicil to his will to this effect. After he was drowned in the *Lusitania*, it was discovered that the codicil had not been witnessed. At that time, 1915, his collection of paintings were on loan to a London gallery. The British refused to hand over the collection. After many years of verbal battle it was agreed (against the last wishes of Lane) that the collection be divided and exchanged every five years. When you visit the Gallery, you will see a magnificent portrait of Sir Hugh and his sister and the stained-glass windows of Harry Clarke, Evie Hone, James Scanlon and Wilhelmina Geddess are a sight for sore eyes. Seek out, too, Corot's 'Landscape with three figures', which, they say, was painted on his death-bed. When George Bernard Shaw left a great financial legacy to the National Art Gallery, he said it was because he learned more there than anywhere else. I know just what he meant. The Municipal Gallery is also a great thinking-place. There is no end to the knowledge to be garnered in it. So do visit it as soon as possible.

Across the Square, behind the iron railings, stand another four figures. These are Oisin Kelly's beautiful 'Children of Lir' changing into swans. They commemorate many of those who died in the long fight for independence.

Number 24 housed the offices of a newspaper *An Claidheamh Soluis*, organ of the Gaelic League. Coláiste Mhuire stands today on the site of Number 25, which was the old headquarters of the Gaelic League, where the plans for Easter Week were first discussed. The turn to the right leads to Granby Lane, where Matt Talbot dropped dead on his way to Mass in Dominick Street Friary.

The Black Church up the hill across Dorset Street, calls to mind the death of the great Dublin poet, Austin Clarke, whose book *Twice Around The Black Church* is another gem. Revolutionary Square, yes, indeed. Vaughan's Hotel at Number 29 was the scene of Black-and-Tan raids and I.R.A. escapes and arrests. Number 31 was the home of the A.O.H. or, to give them their full title, The Board of the Ancient Order of Hibernians Registered Friendly Society. They tried to take away support from the Irish Volunteers in 1913 and yet, when the Easter Rising started, some of the Hibernian Rifles were side-by-side

THE CITY CENTRE

with the rebels.

Number 41 housed the National Foresters and Number 44 the headquarters of the National Volunteers. Look at its doorway which opened and shut on thousands of Irish Republican revolutionaries from the days of Pearse. For some years in the early 1970s, it provided the headquarters for *An Phoblacht*, the Republican newspaper. The offices have now moved to Number 58. Number 44 is at present a Republican shop and Sinn Féin offices. The shop sells all kinds of craft souvenirs and handicrafts, many of them made by Republican prisoners in jails and internment camps. Before he died, Joe Clarke, the 1916 veteran, was often to be found on the premises. He took part in the famous Battle of Mount Street Bridge, which was one of the fiercest battles of the 1916 Rising. Joe Clarke was an activist all his life and was the caretaker of the old Sinn Féin Headquarters in Harcourt Street, the courier of the First Dáil Éireann (21 January 1919) and the publisher of the *Wolfe Tone Weekly*. He spent several terms in jail in his lifetime and was probably the oldest active revolutionary in the world before he passed away at ninety-four years.

Yes, the Square is a far cry from the days when each house provided a town residence for the gentry and nobility. Yet many of the elegant doorways and some ornamental plasterwork remain to remind us of those far-off days.

A Note on Publication

Me *Jewel and Darlin' Dublin* was written by Éamonn MacThomáis while he was imprisoned in Mountjoy for membership of the IRA. It was the first ever publication by The O'Brien Press and was an immediate success upon its release in 1974. An updated edition came out in 1975, and it was reprinted a further six times over the years.

In 1994, a revised twentieth-anniversary edition was produced, with new introductions by Michael O'Brien, Publisher, and the author, in which they reminisced about the circumstances of the book's first printing. This time, Éamonn MacThomáis was able to attend the book's launch – he had been in

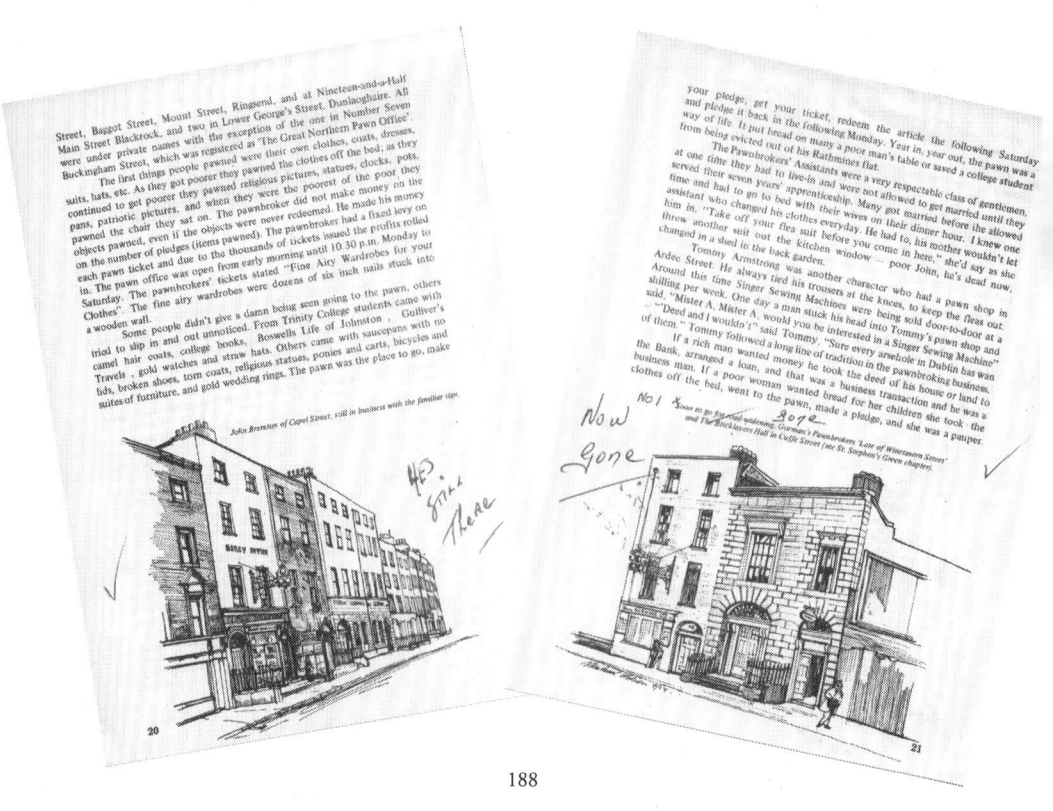

[Handwritten at top: Change photo for new one of a Big Queue for the Savoy —]

crooks all got a hiss and a boo. We hated Love Pictures, but liked Gene Autry, Tom Mix, Roy Rogers, Buck Jones and Tarzan the best, because they never kissed girls. No matter how tough the fight, Gene Autry never lost his hat — and he could kill twelve Indians with one shot out of his gun.

Best for laughs were Wheeler and Wolsey, Charlie Chaplin, The Keystone Cops, Pop-Eye and his girlfriend Olive Oil, and Laurel and Hardy ("This is another nice mess you got me into Stanley"). Although we hated girls Shirley Temple was different and we all saw "The Little Princess" three times. Dublin had its own Shirley Temple contest, and a little girl from the road where I lived was in the first ten.

The outstanding greats of those days were 'Boys' Town', Mickey Rooney, Spencer Tracey, The Dead End Kids in 'Angels with Dirty Faces', James Cagney and 'The Roaring Twenties', 'The Bolero' with George Raft, 'Northwest Passage', 'Mr. Stanley and Dr. Livingstone', 'Jesse James', 'The Daltons Rode Again' and 'Charlie Chan'. We also loved Peter Lorre in detective pictures 'Murder at the Wax Museum' and the wonderful singing pictures of Nelson Eddy and Jeanette McDonald.

The local cinema was more than a picture house, it was a community centre, a place to kill a few hours, something to look forward to, a chance for your mother to wear her new hat, a university of conversation, because whoever saw the picture first would come home and tell the whole road about it.

Left and above: Éamonn MacThomáis's handwritten annotations for the 1994 edition, marking businesses and buildings that were still in use in 1994, or that had closed in the twenty years since the first edition.

189

prison in Portlaoise when the first edition came out, and in his absence, the book was launched by his wife Rosaleen in The Stag's Head on 15 November 1974.

The 1994 text was slightly reshaped by MacThomáis. In his own inimitable voice, he updated the status of some of the markets, pawn shops, newspapers and so on. In this fiftieth-anniversary edition, we have enhanced the book's layout and used MacThomáis 1994 text.

We are delighted to bring you this fiftieth-anniversary edition, with new Forewords by Ivan O'Brien of The O'Brien Press and author and historian Donal Fallon. Step back in time and let Éamonn MacThomáis, fabled raconteur and aficionado of Dublin, bring you on a series of walks around the city he loved so well.

Index

Illustrations are indicated by page numbers in **bold**.

A
Abbey Presbyterian Church, 184
Abbey Street, 60, 64
Act of Union, 167, 179
Adam and Eve's Church, 105
Adam and Eve's tavern, 105
Adelaide Road, 167
Ailred the Dane, 72–3, 105
Ailred's Liberty, 72–4
Aldborough House, **135**, 135
Alexandra College, 166
'All Parcels', 49
Allen, John, 104
almanacs, 63
Ambassador Cinema, 18, 182
Amiens Street, 28, 65, 136
Amiens Street railway station, **122**
Ancient Guild of Incorporated Brick and Stonelayers' Trade Unions, 168–9
Ancient Order of Hibernians (AOH), 186–7
Andrews, Francis, 175
Anglesea Markets, 120
Annals of the Four Masters, 137, 142
Annals of Ulster, 175
Anne, Queen, 124
Apothecaries Hall, 138
Arbour Hill, 94
Ardee Street, 28, 79
Ardilaun, Arthur Edward Guinness, Lord, 159
Armstrong, Tommy, 30–1
Armstrong, Warnesford, 160
Arran Quay, 93
art galleries, 185–6
Ashe, Thomas, 71, 141
Ashtown Road, 185
Astronomical Observatory, Dunsink, 175
Augustinian Church, John's Lane, 36, 73, 105, 112
Augustinian order, 73, 105
Augustus, Emperor of Rome, 32
Aungier Street, 130
Austin, John, 77
Australia, 160
Aylward, Margaret, 78

B
Back Lane, 131
Back of the Pipes, 109–12
Baggot Street, 28, 165
Baily Lighthouse, 60
Balfe, Michael, 161
Balfe Street, 161–2
Ball, Walter, 164
ballads, 45, 49, 51–2, 80, 92, 95, 161, 178, 185
Ballast Office clock, 44, 175–6
Balloon Man, 120
Ballsbridge, 57
Ballybough, 137, 163, 179
Banba Hall, 185
'Bang Bang', 40–2, 79
Bank of Ireland, 179–80
Barbers' Hall, 161
Bark Kitchen pub, 95
Barnardo's Children's Homes, 116
Barnardo's of Grafton Street, 115
'Barrack Room Ballads' (Kipling), 95
Barrett, Dick, 103–4
Barrington, Sir Jonah, 167, 180
Barry, Kevin, 101, 104, 141, 178
Barry's Hotel, 184
Beaver Street, 84
Becket, Thomas, 69
Bective Abbey, Co. Meath, 70
Beggar's Opera, The (Gay), 107
Behan, Brendan, 143, 158, 160, 169, 179
Belfast, 130–1
Bellew, Mary, 101
Belvedere College, 37, 184
Belvedere Hotel, 184
Benedictine order, 101, 128
Beresford, Lord George, 176
Beresford, John, 123, 156
Beresford Lane, 122
Berkeley Road, 142
Bessborough Avenue, 139

ME JEWEL AND DARLIN' DUBLIN

Bewley's coffee shops, 59, 160
Bibby, Fr Albert, 100, 104
Bird Market, 119
Bird's Nest Orphanage, 146
Bishop Street, 28, 57
Black and Tans, 49, 91, 123, 138, 164, 167, 169, 185, 186
Black Bull Inn, 71–2
Black Church, 186
Blackhall Place, 94
Blackpitts, 78, 114
Blackrock, 28
Blackrock College, 37
Blackwell, John, 83
Blacquiere Bridge, 148
Blacquiere's Liberty, 147–8
Bligh, William, 124
'Blight' (Gogarty), 184
Blind Quay, 116
Bloody Bridge, 96
Blue Coat School, 94
'Bohemian Girl, The' (Balfe), 161
Boland, Harry, 167
Bond, Oliver, 36, 52, 91, 99–100
Book of Armagh, 175
Book of Durrow, 175
Book of Kells, 174–5
Book of Leinster, 175
Boot Lane, 130
Boss Croker tavern, 93
Bow Lane, 96
Bow Street, **56**
boxing, 42–3, 48, 77
Boxing World, 65
Boyle, Margaret, 78
Boyne, Battle of the, 102, 133, 180
Brabazon, William, 71, 74

Brady, Joe, 145
Brazen Head tavern, 36, 91
Brereton's pawnbrokers, **29**
Brian Boru, 83, 148
Brian Boru Harp, 175
Brickfields, 24, 109
Bricklayers' Hall, 168
Bride Street, 28, 119, 163, 169
Bridewell, 97–9, **98**
Bridge Street, 36, 90–2
Bridgefoot Street, 71
Bristol Buildings, 87
Broadstone railway station, 102
Brown, Julia, 101
Browne, Nasan, 151–2
Brugha, Cathal, 104, 167
Buckingham Street, 28, 136–7
Budget, 63
Bull Alley, 42, 76
Bull Island, 124
Bull Wall, 124–5
Bully's Acre, 148–9, 150, 152
Bunting, Edward, 184
Burgh Quay, 121
Burke, Edmund, 93, 100, 171, 174
Burke, Thomas Henry, 43, 145
Burns, Robert, 82
Butler, Lady Eleanor, 139–40
Butler, James, Duke of Ormonde, 149
Butler, Mrs., 163
Butt, Isaac, 123, 143
Butt Bridge, 89, 123
Byrne, Tony, 16

C

Caffrey, Luke, 51–2
Caffrey, Nell, 52
Caffrey, Thomas, 145
Camac river, 21
Camden Market, 119
Camden Street, 16, 115
Cameron, Charles, 111, 139, 158
Capel, Arthur, 132
Capel Street, 28, **29**, 59, 120, 129, 130, 132, 133–4
Capel Street Bridge, 89
Capuchin Friary, 100
card games, 23–4
Carey, James, 138
Carmelite Church, Whitefriars Street, 79, 130
Carmelite order, 79, 130
Carmichael, Ricard, 84
Carmillion, Bartholomew, 182
Carroll, Mary, 140
Carson, Sir Edward, 94
Carsoni, Edward, 94
Carton's of Halston Street, 117
Carton's of Smithfield, 117
Cassells, Richard, 181
Castle Hotel, 184
Castle Market, 119
Castle Street, **86–7**, 87–8
Castleknock, 175
Castletown House, Celbridge, 85, 142, 146
Cat and Cage tavern, 144
Catholic Bulletin, 65
Catholic Emancipation, 93
Cattle Market, 117, 120, **121**

INDEX

Cavendish, Lord Frederick, 43, 145
Cavendish Row, 184
Ceannt, Éamonn, 111
Celbridge, Co. Kildare, 85, 142, 146, 180
Chambers, Sir William, 176, 185
Chance, Oliver, 96
Chancery Street, 97
Channell Row Convent, 101
Chapel Royal, Dublin Castle, 86, 89
Chapelizod, 67, 73, 146, 149
Chaplin, Charlie, 16, 35
Chapter House, St Mary's Abbey, **126**, 129, 134
'Charladies' Ball, The' (O'Dea), 37–9
Charlemont, John Caulfeild, 1st Earl, 185
Charlemont House, 185
Charlemont Mall, 28
Charlemont Street, 64
Charles I, 99
Charles II, 94, 149
Chatham Street, 160
Chesby's glass-house, 179
Chester, 113
Chichester, Sir Arthur, 179
Childers, Erskine, 104
'Children of Lir' (Kelly), 186
Christ Church, Liberty of, 81–3
Christ Church Cathedral, 51, 75, **80**, 81–3, **82**, 106, 110, 111, 115, 128, 169
Christ Church Hill, 79
Christmas Markets, 119–20
Church Lane, 180

Church Street, 90, 97, 99
Church Street Bridge, 89–90
cigarette cards, 26
cinema, 15–19, 182
Cistercian order, 128
city charter, 80
City Fathers, 80, 81, 109
City Hall, 89, 131
city walls, 73, 79–80, 92–3, 105
Civil Service Union, 97
Civil War, 103–4
An Claidheamh Soluis, 186
Clanbrassil Street, 28
Clare, John Fitzgibbon, Lord, 165–6
Clarendon, Henry Hyde, 2nd Earl, 88
Clarendon Street, 160
Clarke, Austin, 186
Clarke, Harry, 186
Clarke, Joe, 137, 167, 187
Clarke, May, 115
Clarke, Tom, 64–5, 136, 183
Clement III, Pope, 73
Clergy's Daughters' School (CDS), 166
Clonliffe, 80, 128, 129
Clonliffe Road, 84
Clonmel, John Scott, 1st Earl, 167
Clontarf, 83–4, 123, 136
Clontarf, Battle of, 83, 105, 148
Clontarf, Pool of, 123
Clontarf Castle, 83, 132
Clontarf Island, 84
Clunlif Gill Moholomoc, 127–8, 129
Coady, James, 160
Cockney rhyming slang, 53

Colbert, Con, 79
College Green, 19, 43, 60, 117–18, 157, 176–81, **177**
College of Surgeons, 46, 116, 158, 170
Collins, Michael, 49, 167
Collins Barracks, 95
Colonia palace, 74–5
Columba, Saint, 174
Comet, 60–3
Commercial Union, 118
Comyn, John, 74–5
Conciliation Hall, 121–2
Conn of the Hundred Battles, 106
Connolly, James, 64, 71, 74, 122, 123, 183
Connolly, Lady Louisa, 85
Conquer Hill, 83
Constitution Hill, 102
Convent of the Holy Faith, 78
Cook Street, 105
Cooley, Thomas, 103
Coombe, the, 28, 35–6, 43, 74, 76, 78–9, 116
Coombe Hospital, **78**, 78–9
Cooper's horse dealers, 57, **59**, 94
'Copper Face Jack' see Clonmel, John Scott, 1st Earl
Coppolo's ice-cream parlour, 20, 168
Córas Iompair Éireann (CIÉ), 95
Cork Hill, 131
Cork Street, 76
Corn Exchange, 121
Cornmarket, 91
Corot, Camille, 186

Corporation Street, 114
Correspondent, 60
Court Laundry, 167–8
Cowley Place, 142
Crane Lane, 67, 116
Crane Street, 111
Crawley, Katto, 52
Croke Park, 56, 184
Cromwell, Christopher, 84
Cromwell, Henry, 146
Cromwell, Oliver, 83–4, 88, 123, 160
Cromwell, William, 84
Cromwell's Court, 84
'Croppies' Hole', 95
Crumlin, 43, 47
Cúchulain, 90
Cuckoo Lane, 130
Cuffe Lane, 115
Cuffe Street, 20, 28, 155, 168–9
Cullenswood, 45–6
Cumberland Street, 139
Curley, Dan, 145
Curragh, Co. Kildare, 42
Curran, C.P., 182
Curran, John Philpot, 165
Custom House, 60, **122**, 123, **124**, 169

D
Daily Express, 66
Daily Market, 119
Daily Sketch, 65
Daisy Market, 58, 112, 120
Dalkey, 123
Dalymount Park, 55
Daly's Club, 157, 180
Dame Court, 131, 171
Dame Street, 59, 64, 67, 87, 111, 117–18
Damer Hall, 158

Dandelion Market, 119
Davis, Billy, 48–9
Davis, Thomas, 64, 84, 145, 165, 174, 179, 185
Dawson, Joshua, 161
Dawson Street, 155, 161
de Blacquiere, Sir John, 147–8
de Clare, Basila, 70
de Clare, Richard (Strongbow), 70, 82, 146, 149
de Cogan, Myles, 70
de Lacy, Hugh, 70, 83
De Libertate Civitatis Dublini, 80
de Phepoe, Adam, 83
Dean Street, 82
Dean's Liberty, 76–9
'Dear Man, The', 45
Debtors' Prison, 71, 123, 143
Dervogil, 127–8, 129
Devlin, Anne, 74, 152
Devlin's clay pipes, 115
Diamond, 65
Dickens, Charles, 96
Dickens, Charles, Jnr., 162–3
Dilke, Sir Charles, 150
Dillon, Sir James, 32
Dillon, John Blake, 64, 145
Dr Steeven's Hospital, 95–6
Dodd and Sons, 117
D'Olier family, 165
D'Olier Street, 63, 65, 119, 178
Dolphin's Barn, 16, 17, 71, 111
Dolphin's Barn Brickworks, 114–15
Dollymount, 84

Dominican order, 101, 104
Dominick, Saint, 104
Dominick Street, 28, 67, 186
Donn of Cooley, 89–90
Donnelly, Dan, **42**, 42–3, 77
Donnelly's Hollow, 145
Dorset Street, 28, 65, 186
Douglas, Shirley, 50
Dracula (Stoker), 163
Drew, Ronnie, 164
Drimnagh, 43, 156
Drogheda, Co. Louth, 110
Drumcondra, 128, 144
Drumcondra Hospital, 144
Dublin Bread Company, 155
Dublin Castle, 64, 74, 86, **87**, 89, 91, 102–3, 132, 151–2, 169, 181
Dublin Chronicle, 60
Dublin Corporation, 25, 32, 84, 94, 106, 111, 120, 124, 160
Dublin Evening Post, 60
Dublin Fire Brigade, 118
Dublin Gazette, 67
Dublin Horse Show, 57, 168
Dublin Intelligence, 63
Dublin Japan Works, 115
Dublin Journal of Medical Science, 138
Dublin Penny Journal, 60
Dublin Port, 60, 121–5, **122**
Dublin Pure Ice Company, 115
Dublin Total Abstinence League, 169
Dublin University Magazine, 67

INDEX

Dublin Zoo, 56, 145
Dubliners, the, 164
'Dublin's Hell', 81–2
Dudley, Thomas see 'Bang Bang'
Duff, Frank, 78
Duffy, Charles Gavan, 64, 145
Duffy, Edward, 166
Duke Street, 37, 160
Dun Laoghaire, 28, 123
Dundalk, Co. Louth, 37

E
Earl of Meath's Liberty, 71–2
Earl Street, 49, 132
Earlsfort Terrace, 155, 166–7
East Arran Street, 120, 130
East Wall Road, 113
Easter Rising, 63, 65, 79, 91, 94, 97, 100–1, 104, 111, 121, 122–3, 150, 152, 169, 178, 183, 186–7
Eccles, Sir John, 142
Eccles Street, 142–3
Edict of Nantes, 123
Edinburgh, 37
Edwards, Hilton, 183
1803 Rebellion, 71, 74, 91, 131, 148–9, 151–2
1848 Rebellion, 91, 183
1867 Rebellion, 91, 152, 183
Elizabeth I, 174
Elizabeth Street, 142
Ellis Quay, 28
Ely House, 166
Ely Place, 165–6

Emmet, Robert, 71, 91, 114, 131, 148, 151–2, 170, 174
'Endymion', 43–4, **44**
Ennis, Paddy, 90
Ensor, John, 181
Epworth House, 158
Erne Street, 28
Espinasse, Paul, 110
Essex Bridge, 132
Essex Quay, 132
Essex Street, 113, 132
Eugenius III, Pope, 128
Eustace Street, 97
Evening Herald, 57
Evening Mail, 57, 66–7
executions, 51–2, 64, 71, 90, 97, 100, 104, 105, 130, 145, 149, 153, 164, 165–6, 180
Eye and Ear Hospital, 167
Eye Opener, 63

F
Faddle Alley, 45
Fade, Street, 182
Fagan, Michael, 145
Famine, 139, 140
Fannin & Co., 170
'Fat Mary', 45
Father Mathew Bridge, 89–90
Father Mathew Feis, 101
Father Mathew Hall, 101
Faulkner's Journal, 66
Feinagle, Gregor von, 135
Fenians, 64, 71, 73–4, 123, 131, 136, 141, 152, 160, 161, 163; see also Irish Republican Brotherhood
Field, John, 77
Fifteen Acres, 145

Findlater, Alexander, 184
Findlater's Church, 184
Findlater's Place, 65
Findlater's Wines, 167, 184–5
Fish Market, 58, 120
Fishamble Street, 81, 116
Fishamble Street Music Hall, 100, 106–7
Fisher, Sir Edward, 146
Fitz-Adlem, William, 69
Fitzgerald, Lord Edward, 71, 85–6, 91, 96–7, 130, 163
FitzHarris, James ('Skin the Goat'), 145–6
Fitzwilliam Street, 164
Five Lamps, 134–40, **135**
Flanagan, 'The Bird', 43
Fleet Street, 28, 60, 178
Florence, 32
Food Market, 119
Foot, Lundy, 115
Ford of Hurdles, 36, 89–90, 97, 103, 104
Forty Steps, 96
Foster, John, 179
Foster Place, 179
'Four Corners of Hell', 43, 82
Four Courts, 91, 103–5, **106**
Four Courts Hotel, 97
Four Masters, 137, 142–3
Four Masters Monument, 142–3
France, 77, 91, 123, 163
Francis Street, 16, **17**, 28, 31, 73, 74, 78, 93, 114, 115, 119–20
Francis Street Church, 46
Franciscan order, 32, 74, 142

Freeman's Journal, 60
Freemasons, 139
Fruit and Vegetable Market, **58**, 119, 120
Furry Glen, 145

G

Gaelic Athletic Association (GAA), 55–6
Gaelic League, 186
Gaiety Theatre, 34–5, **40**, 159–60
Gallows Cross, 164
Gandon, James, 103, 123, 179
Gardiner, Luke *see* Mountjoy, Luke Gardiner, Lord
Gardiner Street, 28
Garland of Howth, 175
Gate Theatre, 182, 183
Geddes, Wilhelmina, 186
General Post Office (GPO), 143
Genoa, 32
George III, 86
George's Hill, 130, 131–2
George's Lane, 182
Germany, 32, 114
Gidley, George, 71–2
Gifford, Grace, 152
Gilbert, Sir John T., 134
Gipsy Rose Lee, 152–3
Glasgow, 37
Glasnevin, 81
Glasnevin Cemetery, 46, 71, 104
Glenmalure House pub, 55
Gloucester Street, 138
Glover's Alley, 155, 170
Gogan's shop, 49

Gogarty, Oliver St John, 97–9, 156, 165, 184
Golden Lane, 76, 82
Goldenbridge, 22, 55
Goldsmith, Oliver, 171, 174
Goodbody's cigarette factory, 114
Gorman's pawnbrokers, 26–7
Gough Monument, 144–5
Grafton Street, 43, 49, 112, 115–16, 155, 160–1, 170
Granby Lane, 186
Granby Row, 28
Grand Canal, 55, 114
Grand Orange Hall, 184
Grangegorman, 81, 94
Granville Place, 114
Grattan, Henry, 112, 156, 171, 173, 174
Grattan Bridge, 89
Grattan's Parliament, 179
Gray, John, statue of, 60
Great Expectations (Dickens), 96
Green Street court-house, 130–1, 145, 147
Gregg the jailer, 52
Grey, Hector, 60, 89, 120
Grey Street, **70**
Guild Street, 137–8
Guinness, Arthur, 110–11
Guinness, Sir Benjamin Lee, 157
Guinness Brewery, 57, 96, **108**, 110–11, 112
Gunn Brothers, 159

H

Hafner's sausages, 115
Hall, Henry, 140
Halliday, Charles, 93

Halpin, George, 124
Halston Street, 117
Hammond Lane, 97
Hande, William, 74
Handel, George Frideric, 100, 106–7
Hangman's Lane, 57
Ha'penny Bridge, 47, 60, 89, 120
Harcourt Street, 94, 155, 167, 185, 187
Hardwicke Hospital, 102
Hardwicke Street, 143
Harold's Cross, 71, 76
Hawkins Street, 121
Hawkins Wall, 121
Hay, Patrick, 104
Hay Hotel, 184
Hay Market, 94
Helga, 121
Hell Fire Club, 157
Hemans, Felicia, 161
Henrietta Street, 102, **103**
Henry II, 69, 128
Henry VIII, 104, 132
Henry Street, 35, 119, 132
Heraclius, Patriarch of Jerusalem, 75
Heuston, Sean, 97, 104
Higgins, Francis, 156
High School, Harcourt Street, 167
High Street, 92, 106
Hoey's Court, 88
Hole in the Wall, 149
Holy Faith school, Kilcoole, 36
Holy Ghost Fathers, 37
Home Rule, 94, 143
Hone, Evie, 186
Hope, Jemmy, 77
Horish, William, 131

INDEX

horse racing, 93
hospitals, 40–1, 73, 78–9, 81, 95–6, 102, 132–3, 138, 143, 149, 160, 165, 167, 181–2
Hostage, The (Behan), 143
House by the Churchyard, The (Le Fanu), 67
House of Industry Hospitals, 102
Hovenden Orr, 170
Howth Harbour, 56
Huguenots, 77–8, 88, 97, 110, 123, 164
Hume Street, 155, 165
Hume Street Hospital, 165
Hunter's Brickworks, 114–15
Hutton, Annie, 84, 185

I

Inchicore, 16, 19, 153, 156
Inns of Court, 104; see also King's Inns
Invincibles, 43, 91, 131, 138, 169
Iona, 174–5
Ireland's Own, 65, 66
Irish Builder, 65
Irish Citizen, 65
Irish Citizen Army, 64, 122–3, 158
Irish College, Rome, 91
Irish Direct Trading Company, 170
Irish Felon, 63, 64
Irish Film Centre, 97
Irish Freedom, 64–5
Irish National Union of Vintners', Grocers' and Allied Trades' Assistants, 185

Irish Optical Association, 37
Irish People, 63, 64, 66, 141
Irish Press, 122
Irish Republican Army (IRA), 49, 123, 138, 169, 186
Irish Republican Brotherhood (IRB), 64–5, 131, 136, 141, 161, 163; see also Fenians
Irish Times, 65–6, 178
Irish Times Weekly, 60
Irish Tobacco Company, 115
Irish Volunteer, 64
Irish Volunteers, 64, 182–3, 186–7
Islandbridge Barracks, 151–2
Isolde, Princess of Dublin, 149
Italian immigrants, 53, 94
Italy, 32, 91; *see also* Rome
Iveagh House, 157
Iveagh Market, 93, 112, 119
Iveagh Trust, 53
Ivory, Thomas, 94

J

Jackson, Eleanor, 99–100
Jackson, Henry, 99
Jacob's biscuit factory, 57, 77
Jameson's Distillery, 58, 117
James II, 67, 102–3, 133–4, 175
James's Street, 16, 27–8, 43, 49, 71
Jerusalem, 73, 75, 157
Jervis, Sir Humphrey, 132, 134
Jervis Street, 115, 132–4
Jervis Street Hospital, 132–3
Jesuits, 37, 77, 168

Jews, 78, 175
John, King, 70, 75, 80, 81
Johnny Giles's Market, 112
John's Lane, 36, 42, 73, 74, 105, 112
Johnson, Esther ('Stella'), 180
Johnson, Francis, 86
Johnston, Francis, 143
Johnston's Court, 160
Joly collection, 51
Jones, Henry, 175
Joyce, James, 97–9, 143, 165, 176, 184

K

Kane, Robert, 138–9
Kapp and Peterson pipes, 158
Kavanagh, Patrick, 160, 179
Keane, Henry, 176
Keating, Ellen, 101
Kells, Co. Meath, 50, 175
Kelly, Luke, 164
Kelly, Oisin, 186
Kelly, Paddy, 63
Kelly, Thomas J., 161
Kelly, Tim, 145
Kelly's Cigars, 115
Kelly's Timber Yard, **72**, 73
Kevin Street, 82
Kevin Street Garda Station, 75–6, 78
Kilcoole, Co. Wicklow, 36
Kildare Street, 60, 155, 162–4
Kildare Street Club, 163–4, **164**
Kilkenny Castle, 139
Kilmainham, 16, 22, 57, 83, 148–53

Kilmainham Jail, 52, 100, 104, 149, **150–1**, 152
'Kilmainham Madonna', 152
Kilmainham Priory, 146
Kilwarden, Arthur Wolfe, Lord, 74
King's Hospital School, 94–5
King's Inns, 94, 102, **103**, 104
King's Inns library, 102, **103**
Kipling, Rudyard, 95
Kirwan, Richard, 183–4
Kirwan, Walter Blake, 168
Knights Hospitallers, 83, 149
Knights of Columbanus, 166
Knights Templar, 83
Kreisler, Fritz, 49–50

L
La Touche Bank, **86–7**, 88
Lamb Alley, 92
'Landscape with Three Figures' (Corot), 186
Lane, Sir Hugh, 161, 185–6
Larkin, James, 122
Laurence O'Toole's Church, 137
Le Fanu, Joseph Sheridan, 67
Le Porter, Ralph, 74
Leeson Street, 155, 166
Leeson Street Bridge, 166
Legion of Mary, 78
Leinster House, 163
Leinster Market, 119
Leixlip Castle, 146
Lemon's sweets, 57–9
Liam Mellows Bridge, 94

Liberties, 19, 35–6, 40–2, 45, 49, 53, 57, 69–84, **70**, 90, 114, 119, 150
Liberty Hall, 64, 89, 121, 122
Liberty Market, 119
Liffey, river, 57, 59, 70, 73, 89–90, 96, 105, 121, 128, 132, 152
Liffey Street, 60, 120
Lincoln Place, 176
'Lino', 47–8
Little Elbow Lane, 74
Little Flower Hall, 19
Little Italy, 53
Little John, 90
Llangollen, 139–40
Loftus, Adam, 173–4
Lombard Street, 28
Lombards, 31–2
Longford, Christine, Lady, 183
Longford Street, 82
Loop Line railway Bridge, 123
Lord Edward Street, 46
Lord Mayor of Dublin, 79–81, 109–10, 132, 142, 165, 174
Lord Mayor's Liberty, 79–81
Louis XIV of France, 91
Lover, Samuel, 178
Lowe, William, 183
Lowsie Hill, 109–11
Luby, Thomas Clarke, 64, 136
Lucas, Charles, 100
Lusitania, 161, 185
Luttrell, Thomas, 74

M
McCafferty, Nell, 68

McCall, P.J., 77
McCall's pub, 77
McCartan, Pat, 65
McDaid's pub, 160
MacDiarmada, Seán, 64–5
McDonagh, Thomas, 111, 155
McEvoy, Lilian, 49–50
Mac Fírbis, Duald, 88
McGarrity, J.J., 122
McIntyre, Patrick, 63
McKelvey, Joe, 103–4
McKinley, Peter, 71–2
Mackintosh's chocolate, 57
MacLiammóir, Micheál, 183
McMahon, Hugh Óg, 88, 105
MacMurrough, Dermot, 174
McNally, Leonard, 167
McSwiney, Terence, 65
Madden, Richard Robert, 95
Magan, Francis, 96
Magan, Mary, 96
Magazine Fort, 146
Magee, William, 156
Maguire, Conor, 88, 105
Maguire, Daniel, 114
Mahar, Daniel, 115
Maigned, Saint, 148
Major Sirr's Stag House, 52, 152
Malachi, 127–8, 129
Mallin, Michael, 122, 158
Mangan, James Clarence, 77, 88, 169
Manor Street, 16, 48, 81
Mansion House, 161–2
Marist Fathers, 37
markets, **58**, 81, 89, 93, 112–13, 117, 119–20

INDEX

Markievicz, Constance, 158
Marlborough Street, 28, 49, 131
Marrowbone Distillery, 111
Marrowbone Lane, 71, 111
Marsh, Narcissus, 76–7
Marshalsea Lane, 71
Marsh's Library, **76**, 76–7, 78, 162
Martin, John, 64
Martyrology of Donegal, 137
Mary Street, 16
Mason, Thomas, 116
Mason's Market, 119
Mater Hospital, 142
Meath Hospital, 138, 169
Meath Street, 71
Meath Street Liberties Market, 112
Mee, Giles, 109
Meetinghouse Lane, **126**, 129
Mellows, Liam, 103–4, 153
Mendicity Institution, 96–7
Mercer, Mary, 160
Mercers' Girls' School, 95
Mercers' Hospital, 160, 181–2
Merchant Bar, 91
merchants, 105, 112–19, 124
Merchant's Quay, 103–5, 115, 142
Merrion Row, 155, 164–5
Merrion Square, 67, 110, 155
Merrion Street, 145
Messiah (Handel), 100, 107
Metal Bridge *see* Ha'penny Bridge
Metropole, 19

Millar's Copper and Brass Works, 99
Millenium Park, 116
Milltown, 76
Misery Hill, 71, 125
Mrs Smylie's Homes, 78
Mitchel, John, 63, 64, 131
Mitchell, Thomas, 175
Mitchell's pub, 162–3
Mogh, King of Munster, 106
Moira House, 96–7
Molesworth Hall, **162**
Monto, 82
Monument Creamery, 20
Moore, Henry, 132
Moore, Michael, 175
Moore, Thomas, 142, 174
Moore Street, 35–6, 39, 51, 57, 119, 120, 132, 183
Moran, Michael *see* 'Zozimus'
Morgan, Sydney, Lady, 88, 163
Morgan House Junior School, 95
Mosse, Bartholomew, 181–2
Mother Redcap's Market, 93, 112
Mount Brown Hill, 153
Mount Eccles House, 142
Mount Jerome Cemetery, 77
Mount Street, 28
Mount Street Bridge, Battle of, 187
Mountjoy, Luke Gardiner, Lord, 102, 140–2, 144
Mountjoy Jail, 56, 104, 140–2, 144, 153
Mountjoy Square, 141, **141**
Mud Island, 135
Muldowney's pub, 21

Mullally, Teresa, 131–2
Mullet, James, 91
Mullet's pub, 36, 91
Mullinahack, 74
Municipal Art Gallery, 161, 185–6
Murphy, Nicholas, 71
Murray, John, 37
Murrough mac Briain, 148, 150
Murrough's Cross, 149
Museum of Modern Art, 149–50
music, 41, 49–50, 72, 80, 86, 91, 95, 100, 106–7, 161

N
na gCopaleen, Myles, 179
Nagle, Nano, 78, 131–2
Nation, 63, 64, 143, 145
National Ballroom, 185
National College of Art, 163
National Concert Hall, 167
National Foresters, 187
National Gallery of Ireland, 186
National Library of Ireland, 32, 51, 60, 139, 155, 163
National Liberary Society, 155–6
National Museum of Ireland, 106, 134, 163, 165
National Volunteers, 187
Neilson, Samuel, 63, 130–1
Nelson, Horatio, of Grafton Street, 46
Nelson Street, 143
Netherlands, 32
New Ross, Co. Wexford, 72, 140

New Street, 82
Newcomen Bridge, 139
Newcomen's Bank, 88
Newgate Cant, 51–2
Newgate Jail, 48, 52, 85, 91, 92, 97, 100, **129**, 130, 160
Newman, John Henry, 167
newspapers, 57, 60–8, **61–2**, 141, 178, 186, 187
Norfolk Market, 112
North Brunswick Street, 102
North Circular Road, 120
North Dublin Union, 102
North Earl Street, 49
North Strand Road, 139
North Wall, 124
Northern Star, 63–4, 130

O
Oats, John, 87
O'Casey, Seán, 133, 184
O'Connell, Daniel, 136
O'Connell Bridge, 89, 121, 155
O'Connell Street, 16, 43, 49, 53, 132, 141, 143, 183, 185
O'Connor, Fr Dominick, 100
O'Connor, Rory, 103–4
O'Curry, Eugene, 137
O'Dea, James, 36
O'Dea, Jimmy, 34–9, **35, 36**, 57, 91, 159–60
O'Dea, Martha, 36
O'Dea, Rita, 37
O'Donnell, Pat, 138
O'Donoghue's pub, 164–5
O'Donovan, Harry, 35–6, 39, 159
O'Donovan, John, 136–7

O'Donovan Rossa, Jeremiah, 64, 131, 136, 140, 166
O'Donovan Rossa Bridge, 89, **106**
O'Keefe, Fr Nicholas, 46
O'Keefe's knackers yard, 57
O'Farrell, Elizabeth, 100
Ogilvy, John, 88
O'Hurley, Dermot, 164
O'Leary, Pagan, 73–4, 137
Oman, Willie, 122
O'Moore, Rory, 90–1, 178
O'Rahilly, The, 64
Orange Order, 88, 184
Orby, 93
O'Reilly, John Boyle, 152
Ó Ríordáin, Breandán, 106
Ormond Quay, 128
O'Ruadan, Felix, 128–9
O'Toole, Adam, 180
O'Toole, Laurence, 69, 74, 83
Our Boys, 66
Our Lady of Dublin statue, 79, 130
Owens, Robert, 183
'Owny the Fool', 45
Oxmantown, 48, 90, 94, 97, 128, 134

P
Pakenham, Catherine Sarah Dorothea, 143
Palace Row, 185
Palace Street, 116, 181
Palmerstown, 73, 94–5
Parke, Robert, 179
Parke's hardware, 116
Parkgate Street, 95
Parliament House, 59, 176–80
Parliament Square, 172

Parliament Street, 64, 66, 89, 115, 116
Parnell, Charles Stewart, 100, 143
Parnell Monument, 60, 183
Parnell Square, 180–7
Parnell Street, 28, 57, 65, 113, 183
Partridge, William, 122
Patrick, Saint, 89–90, 110
Patrick Street, 45, 46, 77, 82
Patrick Street Market, 112
pawnbrokers, 27–34, **29, 30, 31**, 168
Pearl Bar, 178–9
Pearse, Edward Lovett, 179
Pearse, Patrick, 65, 100, 122–3, 155, 183
Pearse Street, 176
'Peg the Man', 45
Pembroke Street, 166
Penn, William, 88
pennies, **19, 20**, 19–21
pest-houses, 81, 84
Peter Street, 84
Peter Street Cemetery, 77
Phibsborough, 17, 81, 94, 148
Philadelphia, 122
An Phoblacht, 63, 141, 187
Phoenix Park, 43, 56, 83, 128, 144–8, 149, 152
Phoenix Park Market, 112
Phoenix Park murders, 43, 145
Phoenix Pillar, 145
Pidgeon, John, 125
Pidgeon House, 125
Pidgeon's sausages, 115
Pill Lane, 97, 98
Pimlico, 64, 71
Pipers' Club, 72

INDEX

Piphoe, Adam, 132
Piphoe, John, 132
Plantation of Ulster, 179
Pleasant Street, 44
Pleasants, Thomas, 79
Plunkett, James, 179
Poddle, river, 76
Poland, 114
police, 21, 23, 49, 136
Ponsonby, Sarah, 139–40
Poolbeg Lighthouse, 124
Poole, Joe, 138
Poor Clare Sisters, 101
Portland Row, 137
Portlaoise Prison, 141, 146
Portobello Barracks, 63
Potato Market, 119
Potter, Maureen, **36**, 39, 159–60
Presentation Sisters, 131–2
'President Keely', 46
Pretty Polly is a Dinger (Stoker), 163
Price, Arthur, 110–11
Primate's Hill, 102
Principles of Freedom (McSwiney), 65
Proclamation, 183
Proud's Lane, 155, 169
Provost Prison, 95, 114
Prussia Street, 120
Public Records Office, 104
pubs, 21, 36, 54, 55, 71–2, 77, 81–2, 91, 93, 95, 105, 110, 112, 160, 162–3, 164–5, 178–9
Pue's Occurrences, 63

Q

Quakers, 78, 88, 97
Queen Street, 28, 57, 94
Queen's Head tavern, 88

R

Racing Judge, 65
Rainsford, Sir Mark, 110
Ram Alley, 51, 80
Ranelagh, 45–6, 169
Rathborne Ltd., 113–14
Rathmines, 73
Rathmines Road, 16
Rawson, John, 83, 146
Read's cutlers, 116, **117**
Red Bank restaurant, 178
Red Cow Lane, **58**
Redmond, Denis Lambert, 149, 151–2
Reformation, 74, 83
Reilly, Thomas Delvin, 64
Reilly's Fort, 101
Repeal Association, 122
Reynolds, Thomas, 91
Rialto, 55
Rialto Bridge, 20
Rice, Alice, 101
Richmond Hospital, **101**, 102
Richmond Jail, 138, 161, 163
Richmond Street, 28
Ringsend, 28, 123, 125
Robb, John, 130–1
Robbers' Den, 21, 96, 109
Robin Hood, 90
Robinson, William, 149
Roddy the Rover, 178
Roman Empire, 32
Rome, 32, 72–3, 91, 128
Rotunda Assembly Hall, 182
Rotunda Gardens, 183
Rotunda Hospital, 40–1, 79, 181–2
Rotunda Round Room, 182–3

Rowserstown, 21, 22
Royal Astronomer of Ireland, 175
Royal Canal, 139, 148
Royal Circus, 140–4
Royal Dublin Society (RDS), 168, 183
Royal Exchange see City Hall
Royal Hospital, Kilmainham, 149–50
Royal Iris, 125
Royal Irish Academy, 162, 184
Royal Irish Constabulary (RIC), 136; see also police
Royal National Lifeboat Institution (RNLI), 121
Royal Society of Antiquaries of Ireland, 155
Royal Way, 144, 166
Ruddle's snuff, 115
Ruskin, John, 73
Russell, Thomas, 130–1
Russia, 114
Ryan's pub, 42, 95

S

Sackville Street see O'Connell Street
St Andrew's Church, 180–1
St Ann's Church, 161
St Ann's school, **162**
St Anthony's Hall, 105
St Audoen's Arch, 72, 105
St Audoen's Church, 36, 79, **83**, 105–6, **107**, 111–12, 169
St Catherine's Church, 41, 69, 71, 112
St Finian's Church, 167

St George's Church,
  Hardwicke Street, 143
St George's Church,
  Whitworth Road, 84, 144
St James's Church, 112
St James's Gate, 57, 96, **108**
St James's Well, 111
St John the Baptist Priory, 149
St John's Well, 151, 152
St Joseph's Night Shelter, 79
St Mary's Abbey, 79, 80, 99, 113, 127–34
St Mary's Church, **133**, 133
St Michael's and John's Church, 106
St Michan's Church, **98**, 100, 104, 132, 148–9
St Nicholas of Myra Church, 31, 74
St Patrick's Cathedral, **75**, 110, 119, 157
St Patrick's Hospital, 96
St Patrick's Park, 76
St Patrick's Well, 74–5
St Paul's Church, 93
St Peter's Church, 94
St Quintin, Richard, 71–2
St Saviour's Priory, 104
St Sepulchre's Liberty, 74–6, **75**, 160
St Stephen's Green, 16, 77–8, 116, **154**, 155–70, **157**, 159
St Thomas's Hill, 146
St Vincent's Hospital, 156
St Werburgh's Church, **85**, 85–8, 113
Salock Woods, 128
Salvation Army, 170
Sanderson, John, 176
Sandwick, 71

Sarah Bridge, 152
Sarsfield Quay, 95
Saul Court Academy, 77
Savage, Martin, 185
Scanlon, James, 186
School of Medicine, 84
schools, 94–5, 131–2, 135, 167
Scoil Éanna, 123
Scotch House pub, 121
Scotland, 37
Seagrave, J., 74
Sean Heuston Bridge, 89, 95
1798 Rebellion, 71, 91, 95, 100, 102, 131, 140, 142, 165–6
Seville Place, 137–8
Shamrock and Emerald, 65
Shaw, George Bernard, 167, 186
Sheares brothers, 100, 130, 160, 165, 167
Sheehy-Skeffington, Francis, 63
Shelbourne Hotel, 156
Sheridan, Edward, 168
Ship Street, 82
Silken Thomas, 74, 129–30, 174
Simnel, Lambert, 83
Sinn Féin, 167, 183, 184, 187
Sinn Féin Rebellion Handbook, 65, 178
Sinnot Place, 65
Sirr, Henry Charles, 52, 86, 91, 114, 131, 152
1641 Rebellion, 88, 90, 105, 178
Skinner's Row, 51, 79
Skippers' Alley, 105
slang, 51–5, 184

Sligo, 88
Smith, Erasmus, 167
Smith, Thomas, 174
Smith and Sheppard factory, 170
Smithfield, 57, 58, 117
Smock Alley Theatre, 107
Smyllie, R. M., 178
Smyth, Edward, 123, 179
Smyth, John, 176
Socialist Party, 74
South Anne Street, 160
South Circular Road, 76
South Dublin Union, 15
South Frederick Street, 37
South George's Street, 181–2
South King Street, 155, 159–61
South Wall, 124, 125, 138
Spanish Organ, 175
'Specs', 47
Spencer Dock, 138
Spitalfields, 42–3
Spratt, Fr John Francis, 79, 130
Stackpoole, Margaret, 169
Stafford Street, 133
Stein's sausages, 115
Stella *see* Johnson, Esther ('Stella')
Stephens, Davy, **50**
Stephens, James, 136, 161, 163
Stephen's Street, 82
Stewart, Richard, 86
Stoker, Bram, 163
'Stoney Pockets', 45, 46
Stoneybatter, 113
Stormont, 94
Stratford, Edward, 135

INDEX

Stratford-on-Slaney, Co. Wicklow, 135
street characters, 40–51, 78–9
street games, 21–6
street musicians, 49–50
Strongbow see de Clare, Richard
Stump's sausages, 115
Suffolk Street, 180–1
Sullivan, A.M., 64
Summerhill, 28, 136
Sun Insurance Company, 118
Sutton, 84
Sutton Creek, 84
sweets, 20, 57–9
Swift, Jonathan, 77, 88, 174, 180
Swift Museum, 96
Synnot Place, 142

T

Tailors' Hall, 92–3, **93**, 131
Táin Bó Cúailnge, 90
An Taisce, 102
Talbot, Matt, 48, 139, 186
Talbot Street, 16, 28
Tallaght, 76
Tandy, Napper, 86, 91, 147, 182
Tara, Co. Meath, 90
Taylor's snuff, 115
Telford and Telford organ-builders, 115
Temple Street, 143–4
Temple Street Children's Hospital, 143
theatre, 34–9, **36**, **40**, 107, 159–60, 182, 183
Theatre Royal, 49–50
Thingmote, 180, 181
Tholsel, 80, 81
Thomas Court and Donore, Liberty of, 69–70, 76, 128
Thomas Street, 41, 49, 69, 71–4, **72**, 111, 119, 134
Thom's Directory, 65
Thundercut Alley, 94
'Tie-Me-Up', 47
Tit-Bits, 65
Tivoli Theatre, 16, **17**
Tolka river, 80, 128
tolls, 81, 89, 104
Tomkins, Bobby, 46
Tone, Theobald Wolfe, 95, 106, 133, 160, 161, 174
Town and Country Club, 182
trade guilds, 79, 168–9
Trinity College, 29, 44, 59, 67, 82, 93, 94, 113, 114, 131, 170–6, **171**, **172**
Trinity Street, 64
Turkish baths, 170
Tyburn, London, 105, 130
Tyrone House, 131
Twice Around the Black Church (Clarke), 186

U

Ulysses (Joyce), 97–9, 143, 165
Union Morgue, 26
Unitarian Church, 158
United Irishman, 63, 64
United Irishmen, 63, 72, 77, 92, 99–100, 102, 130, 182
United States, 43, 100, 122
University College Dublin, 166
Usher's Island, 96–7
Usher's Quay, 97

V

Vanhomrigh, Vanessa, 180–1
Vaughan, Honora, 101
Vaughan's Hotel, 186
Vernon, Sir George, 83
Vernon, John, 83–4
Vicar Street, 73, 74
Vicar Street Guardhouse, 74
Viceregal Lodge, 145
Victorine Canons, 69
Vienna, 32
Viking Dublin, 106, 163

W

Walkinstown, 43
Walsh, Rev. Nicholas, 88
War of Independence, 49, 91, 123, 138, 164, 169, 185, 186
Ward's Hill, 57, 77
Ware, James, 85, 87–8
Warren, Siki 'Cyclone', 48
Watkins' Brewery, 79
Watling Street, 96
Weafer's pawnbrokers, **31**
Weaver, Elizabeth, 101
Weavers' Hall, 77
weddings, 25, 46
Wellington, Arthur Wellesley, 1st Duke, 143, 145
Wellington Monument, 145
Werburgh Street, 87
Wesley, John, 78, 96
Wesley College, **157**, 157–8
West, Robert, 182
Westland Row, 110, 176
Westmoreland Street, 175, 179

West's jewellers, 115–16
Wexford, 66, 72, 136, 142
Whaley, Buck, 157
Whateley, Richard, 156
whippings, 89, 131, 151
White Bull Inn, 71
Whitefriars Street, 79, 130
Whitworth Hospital, 102
Whyte's Academy, 160
Wicklow Street, 161, 170–1
Wide Streets Commissioners, 116
Wilde, Oscar, 176
Wilde, Sir Robert William, 143
William of Orange, 32, 133, 180
Willwood jams, 57
Winetavern Street, 28, 81, **106**
Winetavern Street Bridge, 89, 106
Witherington, Matilda, 160
Woffington, Peg, 107
Wolfe Tone Weekly, 63, 187
Wolsey, Thomas, 136
Wood Quay, 106, 149
Woods, Stanley, 144
Workers' Republic, 64
Workmen's Club, 169–70
Wormwood Gate, 91
Writers' Museum, 185

Y

Yeats, W.B., 167
Yellow Bottle Inn, 72
Yelverton, Barry, 147
York Street, 155, 169
Youkstetterr's sausages, 115
Young Irelanders, 64, 71, 121–2, 131, 185

Z

Zekerman, Andreas, 71–2
'Zozimus', **45**, 45–6, 49, 51, 52, 64
Zozimus, 63, 64

Enjoying life with

O'BRIEN

Hundreds of books
for all occasions

From beautiful gifts to books you'll want to keep forever! Great writing, wonderful illustration and leading design. Discover books for readers of all ages.

Follow us for all the latest news and information, or go to our website to explore our full range of titles.

TheOBrienPress   TheOBrienPress
OBrienPress   TheOBrienPress

Visit, explore, buy
obrien.ie